THE GREEN
FIRE

THE GREEN
FIRE

KANIKA ADLAKHA

Published Internationally by

 **Pendown** Press

Powered by G Gullybaba.com

PENDOWN PRESS

Powered by Gullybaba Publishing House Pvt. Ltd.,

An ISO 9001 & ISO 14001 certified Co.,

Regd. Office: 2525/193, 1st Floor, Onkar Nagar-A, Tri Nagar, Delhi-110035, (From Kanhaiya Nagar Metro Station Towards Old Bus Stand)
Branch Office: 1A/2A, 20, Hari Sadan, Ansari Road, Daryaganj, New Delhi-110002
Ph.: 09350849407, 011-27387998
E-mail: info@pendownpress.com
Website: PendownPress.com

First Edition: 2020

ISBN: 978-93-90116-94-2

Layout Design: Pendown Press Publishing

This book is dedicated to my maternal grandfather–Late Shri Ishwar Chand.

It is based on the true life incidents that he faced during India's partition.

"It is never late to ask yourself "Am I ready to change my life, am I ready to change myself?" However old we are, whatever we went through, it is always possible to be reborn. If each day is a copy of the last one, what a pity! Every breath is a chance to be reborn. But to be reborn into a new life, you have to die before dying."

–Shams Tabriz

"It is impossible to discourage the real writers-they don't give a damn what you say, they're going to write."

–Sinclair Lewis

CONTENTS

PART-II

PREFACE

I have grown up listening to the numerous stories of partition told by my grandfather and grandmother. These stories were sometimes bitter and sometimes nostalgic of the happy times spent in Pakistan.

When I searched for the books on partition, I found many such books which narrated the horror of partition. But none of them addressed the problem of refugees settling into "Hindustan".

These homeless people were not welcomed with open arms.

They faced many hardships and had to start everything from a scratch. It is really praiseworthy that in spite of being robbed off literally of all material possessions, they not only survived bravely but also respectfully.

These penniless and homeless people never succumbed to illegal practices or degraded themselves to begging or looting. Rather they worked really hard to earn back their lost pride and respect in this new country.

Perhaps these were the only people who cried when India rejoiced in its newly found freedom. They indeed paid a heavy price to win this independence in 1947. It won't be wrong to call them martyrs of independence.

No one community or religion is to be blamed for what occured during partition. When the people of east and west Punjab were brought down to their knees... families were murdered in cold blood; loot and anarchy was common. Those who survived thought themselves to be lucky.

This is just not another book on partition. It is the source of inspiration for today's generation to never ever give up on life and how to survive in the worst conditions.

ACKNOWLEDGEMENTS

I am thankful to **Manuj Adlakha**, my husband, for always encouraging me to write. Giving me new ideas and insights and keeping up the motivation of writing.

Jayant Adlakha, my son, for keeping me positive and happy.

All the strong and supportive people in my life; Amma, Mummy, Papa, my mother-in-law, Mama, my sisters, cousins, aunts and my Brother

My favourite authors: **Robin Sharma, Jane Austen, Rhonda Byrne**

My inspirational character: **Shams** of **Tabriz,** who made **Rumi** a poet from a scholar; his teachings inspired me to write and publish this book; long after I had totally given up. (courtesy of Forty Rules of Love)

My publishers: The entire team of **GullyBaba**, especially **Ritu** and **Dinesh Verma** for their round the clock support.

My alma mater: Our Lady of **Fatima** Convent, Gurugram and Writers Bureau, UK for bringing out the writer in me.

And Finally but immensely, Pitaji (my maternal grandfather) for those long interviews about partition.

Thank you all for being there for me.

Part–I

Chapter 1

NWFP

It was a rather colder October morning than usual. Balraj Dass had just been back from the old Shiva temple in Chitti Gatti near Mansehra. The winter was already knocking doors in the northern province. He was a big devotee of Lord Shiva. Every year in February, during the Mahashivratri festival, he would eagerly volunteer for the Sewa (service) of pilgrims coming from as far as Punjab and Delhi. The north western frontier province where he lived was one of the most beautiful areas of the world, located on both sides of the Indus river, lazily stretching from cool Himalayas in the north to the hot desert like Baluchistan and Punjab in the south. To its west was the famous Khyber Pass through the Koh Suleiman range bordering Afghanistan.

This mountainous region was inhabited by Pathans who had not been bowed down by any ruling power. Balraj Dass had made many Pathan friends with whom he animatedly discussed the latest political developments. Shabbir was one such friend, whom he thought well read. Shabbir was an avid traveler. He had been to the snow-capped mountains of Chitral, its lush green valleys and scenic beauty, the Khyber pass, the exotic route from Peshawar to Kabul or the hot temperatures of Dera Ismail Khan, he had experienced it all. For Balraj Dass, Shabbir was a sort of encyclopedia. Often the two discussed the historic importance of Khyber Pass.

The Shiva temple, where they had met for the first time, was thousands of years old. It dated back to the time of king Asoka. Shabbir's knowledge about the history of the province had impressed him a lot. It was Shabbir who told him that the North West Frontier province or NWFP as the Britishers call it was once the heart of Gandhara Kingdom. In the days of Kushan kings it was called the Lotus land. The Gandhara territory had stretched from Peshawar to Taxila. Many invaders came from central Asia through this route to gain entry into India.

The first being Alexander; followed by Kanishka, Pukhtoons, Babar, Nadir Shah and Durrani from Afghanistan. Later, it was taken over by Sikhs then by Britishers finally in 1849. In the same year, the districts of Hazara, Peshawar, Kohat, Bannu, Dera Ismail Khan, Khyber and Khurram were removed from the Punjab administration and areas of Dir, Swat and Chitral were added. This led to the formation of a new province in 1901 named as NWFP (The North-West Frontier Province). It was governed by a British agent to who served under the Governor General. This executive was in direct communication with the Government of India and foreign department. Their headquarters were in Peshawar. Britishers had separated it from the rest of Punjab in 1901 and named it NWFP.

For decades, Hindus and Muslims had been living peacefully together in this beautiful land, but since a few months, many prominent leaders had been visiting this peaceful place, polluting the minds of innocent tribes and slowly creating a rift between Hindus and Muslims. Both the communities grew more and more suspicious of each other with each passing day. It was clear that partition was on its way. But, the thing which was still unclear was-which side will they go The Indian side lead by Congress or the Pakistani side lead by Muslim League—or a separate state of Pashtunistan which was at the heart of every resident of NWFP? The Pathans could not trust the Britishers after 1930-the year when British troops had opened fire on a Muslim gathering at Qissa Khwani and Kalan Bazaar Peshawar. About 300 Pathans had been killed mercilessly in one day. Their only hope was "Sarhadi Gandhi" or Khan Abdul Gaffar Khan and his Khudai Khidmatgars. Mahatma Gandhi had visited twice and he fully supported Abdul Khan Aka Badshah Khan or Bacha Khan, as he was lovingly called.

Today was 10th of October of the year 1946 and Nehru was expected to visit NWFP. Balraj Dass was accompanied by Shabbir and they had specially travelled to Peshawar to have a glimpse of him. They were unaware that today they would become a part of history, representing the crowd that attacked his car.

The crowd was getting impatient. The Mahsud Jirga had assembled on the residency lawn to hear what Nehru had to say. The Pathans would have preferred an Englishman or at least a soldier who could be their leader or representative. Pathans were a tribe of very brave soldiers and they preferred strong men as their rulers. A politician who was totally unaware of military rules of warfare was not acceptable to them.

3

They had been warriors and protectors of this very important land which served as a passage to India. They had been undefeatable tillthen.

Shabbir said in a grave voice as if he had anticipated what was going to happen, "The Pathans bow their heads to no man regardless of rank or lineage, whether it is Afghans or Britishers, we are an independent tribe, and we don't belong to Congress or league. A Pathan asks only one thing of the outside world...'

"What is that?" Balraj Dass asked looking worried.

"To be left alone" Shabbir replied firmly.

As was a tradition customary in the Jirga, that every member was squatting down on the ground in front of the chairs on which only the prominent leaders were seated. Nehru had paid visit to that place without the proper preparation. He had not bothered to study or seek advice regarding the customs of Jirga which was a very important consensus for all the leaders who had assembled from faraway places.

Suddenly, he rose to his feet and advanced to the centre with raised hands as though it was a political rally. Pathans were aghast. They clearly understood that Nehru had not cared for their customs. Still they kept quiet,studying carefully his every move and word.

With an alarmingly raised voice he announced, "I have come to free the tribes from the slavery of British imperialism."

"How dare he call us slaves"

"We are not slaves"

The crowd shouted back. All the squatting members of the Jirga looked towards Nehru with disdain. Shabbir and some other Pathans were furious. In front of them was Mehr dil Mahsud.

He appeared to be the eldest in the Jirga. Unable to control his anger against Nehru, he advanced towards Nehru saying, "We are not slaves" adding "come here again and we will circumcise you". Then he stepped forward to hit Nehru.

Though, he was timely stopped from doing so by a political agent of South Waziristan.

Everything went out of control after this and all the members of Mahsud Jirga raged out of camp shouting anti-Nehru slogans.

Even Nehru had not expected this kind of welcome from the people of Peshawar in his wildest dreams. People waved black flags and shouted "Go back Nehru". Balraj Dass could not believe that people would actually attack Nehru's car. He thought that they were upset with him, but stopping his car and misbehaving with him was totally unexpected. Shabbir too was pushed and pulled from every direction. Like a small leaf floating away with the big current of a river, they too were sucked up in the mob that was menacingly moving towards Nehru's car.

On 17th October, Nehru left Peshawar for Malakand. Balraj Dass learnt from the locals that people welcomed him with stones and he even received an injury on his forehead.

The next day all the local newspapers carried this picture on the first page of the incident between Nehru and Mehr Dil mahsud—The latter trying to slap him and being stopped by a political agent.

The situation turned out to be a premonition of the coming disaster. The year was 1947. Mountbatten was the last viceroy of India. His job was to preside over the division of India. For areas like Bengal and Punjab, he decided that the wish of the people of these two states would be sought for or against their inclusion in Pakistan. This was to be done through voting. But sadly, no such privilege was bestowed to the poor tribal people of NWFP. Instead of voting, a referendum was there to determine their fate. Both Mountbatten and Nehru were fully aware that Khudai Khidmatgars were already in majority in NWFP state assembly and there was no need for a referendum.

Bacha Khan wanted NWFP to join India or at least have a third option of forming their own independent state of "Pashtunistan or Pathanistan". Joining Muslim league or Pakistan was never an option for Khudai Khidmatgars. There was an anger against Nehru for not letting NWFP join India. He not only stopped congress or Khudai Khidmatgars from participating in the referendum but also supported Mountbatten's plans of only two options for the referendum; that was either to join India or Pakistan...

The referendum of NWFP was the most shameful farce in the history of partition of India.

"How can the league be defeated in the referendum when there is no other party in its opposition?" Shabbir was angry by this political maneuver.

Balraj Dass could not agree more. "Yes, I agree with you. You know that tribal Pathans are not allowed to vote. Not only have these, the states of Swat, Dir, Amb and Chitral have been refrained from participating in it."

"I don't understand why the Khudai Khidmatgars have abstained from this referendum. Is Bachha Khan still a kid? Doesn't he understand that by making the league the lone contender in this referendum, he is sabotaging the future of Pathans?" Shabbir nearly cried out.

The Khudai Khidmatgars

Asif overheard Shabbir. He was a Khudai khidmatgar and a staunch believer of Badshshah khan aka Bachha Khan.

"Brother, do you really think that Dr. Khan Sahib is so indifferent towards his people that he would let this happen? "Asif asked Shabbir who looked helpless.

Shabbir was taken aback by a stranger who was approaching them.

"Careful, he might be armed..." Balraj Dass said, pulling Shabbir to his side.

"No need to fear me dear brother, I am a Khudai khidmatgar and a believer of non-violence" Asif said, keeping a friendly hand on Shabbir's shoulder. He indicated him to sit down on a nearby rock.

Shabbir and Balraj Dass reluctantly followed him. They were both impressed and afraid of this man who wore only red clothes from top to toe. Now, it was something totally unconvincing that a warrior tribe like Pathan could be non-violent and follow Gandhi's ideology. In reality, it was totally Badshah khan's novel ideology of combining Islam and non-violence; something which had never been thought of before. He was a great leader who was a Gandhian at heart, but he had created this red army keeping in mind the traditional Pushtun codes of behavior.

Shabbir introduced himself and Balraj Dass to Asif.

"My name is Asif and I am a member of the Khudai Khidmatgar an organization, formed by Badshah khan."

"But not everyone in your organization wears red, I have seen some men in Jirga who wore plain clothes", Balraj Dass enquired like an enthusiastic kid.

"Yes, our organization has civil and military wings. Only the people of the military wing wear red uniforms while the civil wing has older and literate people who coordinate with congress committees.

"How can a Pathan follow these ideologies and politics? We are a warrior tribe"; "Shabbir grew somewhat excited.

"Yes, people taunt us, especially our fellow Muslims. They say that we are not 'real' Pathans. They say Pathans fight with arms, not with words. This irritates us a lot but we have vowed that we will stay non-violent in our struggle."

"People call you Surkh Posh because of this red color" Balraj Dass interrupted.

"Yes, this colour is special because it stands against colonialism. Our leader Badshshah khan had set up Khudai khidmatgars as an organization for social reforms-mainly the Afghans. We initially focused on education and elimination of blood feuds which is so common here."

"I remember reading somewhere that in 1937 Badshah khan's brother Khan Abdul Jabbar Khan was elected as the chief minister of NWFP", Shabbir added, showing off his knowledge on political matters.

Asif smiled. "Yes, we call him Dr. Khan Sahib. He has won this year also and has been re-elected as the Chief minister of NWFP", He said.

"You know people make comparisons between Dr. Khan Sahib and Badshah Khan here in Frontier to that of Nehru and Gandhi in India. Both Gandhi and Badshah khan are big crowd pullers; they just can't sit in office and do paperwork. These things are left to Nehru in India and Dr. Khan here." Now it was Balraj Dass to show Asif that he too was well informed.

Shabbir nodded to his friend approvingly.

"Let me tell you a small story which I have heard from my General about Gandhi's visit to Khudai Khidmatgar's office here in Frontier." Asif said.

"Yes brother, go ahead", Shabbir said, getting excited like a child.

"Gandhi personally wanted to meet officers of Khudai Khidmatgars as he approved Badshah Khan's ideology of bringing together Islam and non-violence. But he personally wanted to test his soldiers as they were Pathans-a warrior tribe. Gandhi then asked them one by one if they totally believed in their leader. They replied affirmatively. Then he again asked what they would do if one day Badshah khan decides to change his ideology and embraces violence. One of the officers promptly replied that they could leave Badshah khan, but they could never leave non-violence. This impressed Gandhi very much", Asif said feeling proud. His cheeks were now of the same shade as his uniform,—Red.

"Well, I don't know about you people, but all this has made me very hungry", Shabbir said, interrupting the tense environment.

"Yes, yes brother. I have not eaten a morsel since morning" Balraj Dass joined him as if understanding what he meant. They both winked at each other.

"Will you join us Asif bhaijaan? "Shabbir said in a rather meek tone.

Asif nodded. Even freedom fighters need to fuel their bellies from time to time.

The trio looked for a place where they could satiate the rumbling noises in their bellies.

9

Luckily Shabbir spotted a Pathan who was rolling out hot *Chapatis* on a big *tawa*.

They seated themselves on a wooden bench and looked at the Pathan. Now, it was not a proper dhaba, just a community kitchen of sorts and this Pathan was a great cook who managed this place along with his father and younger brother.

The father was lying on a cot which had dirty bedclothes on it, but he didn't seem to mind much. He was busy smoking his hookah which made a gurgling sound now and then.

When he saw a Khudai khidmatgar, he stood up from his resting place in excitement and called his younger son.

"Pasha... oye Pasheyaaa"

A boy of about 14-15 years came running from the back of the mud hut. He was probably cutting veggies as his hands were still green and wet. He wiped his hands from the corner of his long kurta.

"Ji Abba..." The elderly motioned him towards the guest's direction. He understood without any further word.

"What have you cooked today?" Shabbir was the first one to enquire. The boy looked at his elder brother who was baking his *chapatis*. He quickly washed his hands and wiped them with a cloth.

"We have Dal Bukhara and Murgh Peshawari today", He said with some hesitation as if it was a blunder to prepare only two dishes for that day.

The cuisine of NWFP was untouched by any of its invaders. The dishes were very simple to prepare, mostly made with large pieces of meat and vegetables which were marinated and slow cooked using some specific spices. Yellow chilli powder, mace powder, Kashmiri mirch and cardamom were the main ingredients.

Dal Bukhara was a plant based lentil curry prepared by slowly simmering black lentils with spices, fresh tomatoes and served with butter as topping. Murgh Peshawari on the other hand was a meat based dish, deep fried in a thick wok. Before that, it was marinated a night before in the choicest spices which added a rich gravy to the chicken.

They gobbled up the entire pots of Dal bukhara and Murgh Peshawari which was laid before them with thick *chapatis* freshly prepared by Pasha's brother.

The elderly man came with water glasses himself. "I am Abdul Rahim and these are my sons Altaf and Pasha. I too wanted to be a part of Khudai Khidmatgars but I fractured my foot badly", He said showing his distorted feet.

Asif rose up from his seat and put his hand on the elderly's shoulder. "We need your support; Badshah Khan needs your support."

"We love our leader, we are with Dr. Sahib and Bachha Khan, and we will do whatever he says. We don't trust anybody except him."

"He is amongst us, He understands our problems. Jinnah is a foreigner to us, just as Nehru", his elder son joined the conversation.

"In shah Allah, we will win, either we will join Hindustan or we will have our own Pashtunistan" Asif said raising his fists in the air.

Shabbir and Balraj Dass exchanged looks. It was time to get off from this Asif. Quickly they pressed a few coins in Pasha's hand and bade goodbye to Asif and the elderly man who were still engrossed in an animated discussion.

"I must say goodbye to you my friend..." Balraj Dass said to Shabbir. He was going back to his family in Kot Qaisrani.

"You look worried my friend.. trust Allah, we will save each Hindu in our area if any need arises", Shabbir said, pressing his hands into Balraj Dass's.

"This is our country and we will not let anyone separate us, we are not going anywhere, we are not leaving you", Balraj Dass said hugging Shabbir...

Chapter 2

DERA GHAZI KHAN

I am Sukhdev, Balraj Dass's eldest son. My Baba calls me "Sukkhi". It was one of the most horrible days of my life. I had been hearing about partition for many days. Baba had told me that violence had broken out in Fatehwali and Rindh, where my maternal grandparents lived, but this hatred of partition would reach our beautiful and peace loving village of Kot Qaisrani so soon, was something that was difficult to imagine.

Kot Qaisrani is a part of Dera Ghazi khan district. The Dera Ghazi Khan is located in a strip between the river Indus and Koh Suleman range of mountains separating it from the province of Balochistan. The district of Dera Ismail Khan surrounds it from the north, while the district of Rajanpur is towards its south. The Indus river flows on the east across which lie the districts of Muzaffargarh and Layyah. Loralai and Dera Bugti Districts of Balochistan province lie on the west separated by the Koh Suleman range of mountains. The district is spread over an area of 11,294 sq.km comprising two tehsils of Dera Ghazi khan and Taunsa Sharif.

We were almost caught unawares that fateful day. I remember Baba was sitting on a wooden cot drinking his salted *lassi*; he had just returned from Peshawar a few days back after meeting his friend Shabbir. He was looking a bit upset as he had heard about looting and massacre in the nearby town.

"What is going around? "He murmured to himself.

"*Hain ji*, did you say something?" Bibi said, wiping the forehead with the corner of her *dupatta*. She had been grinding the flour for the evening meal.

"Oye, Bhaganwali, did you hear that violence has broken out in your native village of Fatehwali? do you have any news about your brother? Are they all right?" asked Baba.

"How would I know ji, I hardly move out of the house except in the morning when I fetch water for household chores, have you heard something?" She said, pulling the *dupatta* over her face. Bhaganwali was the mother of his two sons and two daughters, but while talking to her husband, she made sure that her *dupatta* was firmly pulled over her face whenever she stood in front of him.

"God knows what will be our future, this partition is going to uproot us from our very own earth; there has been no *dangal* competition for the last three months. This whole partition thing has spoiled our peaceful lives and entertainment..."

Baba could not stop thinking about the *dangal* competitions which were a trademark of the small village of Kot Qaisrani. Every fortnight a *dangal* used to be arranged by the village head-man Rahim khan who himself had been a *pehelwan*.

14

Baba had a great body and physique. He was over six feet with broad shoulders and a pointed moustache which gave him a wrestler-like look. He had never been involved actively in *dangals*, but he enjoyed watching them with fellow villagers whenever the competition was held in Kot Qaisrani or any neighboring village.

Besides the big competitions, *dangals* were also fought every Friday. The Punjabis of Kot Qaisrani in particular were extremely fond of wrestling and great *"Chhinjs"* or *"Akharaas"* were organized in several places in the open fields where the Punjabi Jatts would display their expert wrestling skills to spectators .

Though the majority of the population of Kot Qaisrani was Muslims, yet these wrestlers were considered as a common property and the whole village would cheer for them whenever the opponent was from some other town or village.

Baba once told me, "Sukhdev, we belong to a family of wrestlers, so build up your stamina; you should eat more food and develop a good body." One of his cousins Amir Chand was a famous wrestler; he was six feet four inches in height and boasted that nobody in the entire village could eat like him. Every day he would take 1 kg ghee, 2 kg almonds and 2 kg of male goat meat besides eating his routine vegetables and *chapatis*. He was under the training of famous wrestler Hazara Singh of Gujranwala.

The second most important and favourite sport after wrestling was the kabaddi. But we children were only interested in the village fairs which were held from time to time and my favourite was the "Amir Shah ka *Mela*" which was organized on Koh Suleman mountain range. This was an eagerly awaited fair where the children enjoyed *"chadols"* or swings, tradesmen went for sale and purchase of different items but Baba was particularly interested about the wrestling competitions which were a major attraction of the event. For three days, every person would engage himself according to his interests as the *mela* had something for everybody.

Koh Suleman was nearly four miles from Balochistan which was inhabited by tribal Muslims. People of the neighboring villages would attend this *mela* with their entire families. Some would use donkeys and horses, but a majority of people were poor and had no option but to walk. It was one event which was eagerly awaited by both the Hindus and the Muslims. This *mela* was always exciting, and for children it meant pure fun. The children played the whole day at the various swings and when they felt hungry, they would rush to their mothers to get a half *Anna* with which they would buy delicacies like *jalebi, balushahi* and *Sohan halwa* prepared in *desighee*. Shree Ram *Halwa*i was a specialist in preparing *Sohan halwa* from crushed wheat and he elaborately decorated it with crushed cashew nuts and almonds.

As is the tradition in Pakistan, most of the rural fairs are organized in the proximity of Sufi shrines, or are held in open spaces. This is the time for rest and recreation of the villagers, when they get a respite from their tough lives.

During the day time, people are entertained by astrologers, hakims, jugglers, snake charmers and men with monkeys. Some of the farmers also brought along pet roosters and partridges for fights and contests. They enjoyed the fight till late in the evening and some people also betted on these fights.

The evening time was in no manner any less energetic than the day, as the men folk would sit together forming a big circle and passing on the hookah as one of them narrated stories of strength, victory or exploration of new lands and people. Some of the more creative ones cracked jokes and everyone enjoyed themselves in this relaxed environment. In the evening, the *halwa*i would prepare a special sweet dish '*halwa*' made of wheat flour, sugar and ghee and completed with a lot of raisins; with the *halwa* the ceremonies of the day were unofficially called off and people would settle to their resting places. This fair would go on for three days and would sometimes stretch to even four days.

We all would feel very bad while returning from the fair as it meant an end to all our activities and no more delicious sweets.

At home the food was hardly elaborate and only contained simple dishes. We ate food twice a day. The meal was of wheat roti with fresh white butter and salted or sweetened *lassi*. It took a lot of time and hard work to prepare food. The wheat had to be first grinded in the *chakki*, the water had to be fetched from a faraway well, the cream of cow's milk had to be churned to prepare butter and *lassi*, and then Bibi took out cow dung cakes from the small store and finally prepared the *chulha*. It took a lot of puffing and created large amount of smoke which caused itching in her eyes while putting the cow dung cakes to flame; but she carried on her work wiping her reddened eyes with the corner of her *dupatta*.

She prepared really big *rotis*. Whenever we had guests at our home, Bibi would prepare special dishes like *kheer*, *halwa*, *chane ki daal* and sometimes chicken. Cooking non vegetarian food was not easy as the flesh has to be cleared, washed and cut into pieces—all this work was done by Baba while Bibi prepared thick gravy for it. Baba bought chicken whenever his uncle from the nearby village would come to meet him; from morning till evening the *chulha* would be occupied in preparing chicken. So, Bibi would go to neighbor's house to prepare *rotis* for the evening.

17

During the winters, we relished the *Gajar ka Halwa*. My sisters grated the fresh carrots and Bibi added the grated carrots in the boiling milk along with nuts; she kept on churning the ingredients slowly with a long metal spoon from time-to-time. It took a lot of time to cook and we kept on peeping inside the kitchen now and then to check how much of it was cooked. Bibi used to get very angry at this and shooed us away hurling sweet abuses.

It was indeed a tough life for women; from morning till evening they had a lot of chores to do and the most tedious one was that of fetching water. Bibi would get up at dawn and grab her two earthen pots to collect water from the village well. It was mutually decided between the Hindus and Muslims that well water would be shared as there were only two wells in our village. One of the wells was at the end of the village near fields and the other one was at the heart of the village, near the big banyan tree where the headmen would meet occasionally. In one of these meetings, it was decided that Hindus could use water from dawn till noon and Muslims could use it from noon till evening and sometimes till night which rarely happened.

The number of Muslim families soon outnumbered the Hindu families, so once again the meeting was called near the big banyan tree. Muslims wanted that they should be allowed to use the well in the morning hours also. But Baba and other Hindus were just not ready for this. In the end it was decided that Hindus will dig their own well which will be exclusively used by them till then the same routine was to be followed.

It was Baba who gave the suggestion that Hindus would build their own well in the big compound of Lala Ram Lal, but it proved to be a very tedious task.

The well was to be dug with hand-aided only by a shovel and another hand tool. As the well was dug by hand so the digger had to be at the bottom of the hole and it was a very dangerous position, because it meant that as soon as he would reach the groundwater level, he had to hold his breath under water to dig. This was really a dangerous task, besides there was always the risk of shifting of mud and the digger could even get buried.

There was no professional digger available at that time, so one of Baba's cousins Chela Ram offered to complete the task. Initially, everything was going in a planned manner and Chela Ram had almost reached the groundwater level when the sudden shifting of mud killed him. It had been almost a month since the work had started and everyone was happy with the progress but it came to an abrupt end and with the sudden demise of Chela Ram, the work was stopped indefinitely.

After two months, the Muslims began to pressurize us again to start with digging but Baba did not want to lose another life. So, this time he decided to call a professional from Badali. It meant that we had to spend a lot of money on his accommodation, besides paying him for his work. But Baba said that he would manage it on his own.

His name was Pandit Mohan Lal and he was a thorough professional and a truly remarkable man. Every day he would get up at the dawn and practice yoga postures. He could hold his breath for a long time and had a very lean but active body. He fed only on raw vegetables, fruits and milk and never drank or smoked. He surprised everyone by completing the task in just one month. So, now the Hindus had their own well and Baba was very happy that he had kept his promise. The *'rahat'* or the earthen wheel was set up to take out water from the well. In other villages, the ox was used to move this wheel but in our village, the 'rahat' was worked upon by men.

One day Baba brought some wood and soon began working on it, chopping and hammering from edges. Nobody knew what he was up to and nobody dared to ask anything. In the evening, he got up from his seat and revealed a big wooden stand.

"Now we are never going to have any water scarcity, look what I have made", he said wiping away his sweat with his sleeve still holding the hammer.

Bibi came out setting the veil on her forehead and putting one corner of the veil in her mouth. She said surprisingly, "A wooden stand for earthen pots! Now I can store more water without worrying about their breaking." It was a strange gift which Baba had given his wife; her eyes shone brightly thanking him silently for all the pain and consideration her husband had shown to her through this gesture.

My routine went on as usual. Every morning Bibi would wake me up after Baba had left for fields. I quickly completed morning chores and really despised the cold bath from the earthen pot. Bibi prepared a big roti from wheat flour with lots of butter spread in the center. This was supposed to be my breakfast but I never had the time to enjoy it. I would just roll up the *roti* and grab my tin case which contained my books, wooden pen, and a wooden board and ran towards the school which was three miles from our home.

I had always admired the beauty of nature and these morning walks gave me immense pleasure as I walked, ran and jumped through the grassy fields. I had one favourite spot in particular. It was a big stone near the road at some height. I just climbed on it and had the most beautiful view of the lush green fields, the sleeping village houses and far away a small patch of river Indus was also visible. I was not sure whether it was Indus or some other small river but I called it my Indus.

The scene became more heavenly during winters as the sweet chirping of birds was mixed with slanted rays of sunlight peeping through the clouded sky.

In spite of spending some quality time at my favourite spot I was seldom late for school as I walked very fast after my 'morning siesta' as if I had been charged by nature itself.

I was an average student at school with some Muslim and some Hindu friends. We had our usual fights and discussions and enjoyed every bit of school life, till the very news of partition shattered my life to pieces.

It was here, in school that I first realized that I was a Hindu, living in a place which was my birthplace, but not my country and the message was clearly given...violently.

Chapter 3

KOT QAISRANI

It was the darkest day of my life. I had never thought that my rosy world would suddenly turn to a thorny nightmare. I could see tension on everyone's face though people still had faith on their English Sahibs.

The school was closed as the principal had decided to take precautionary measure in this period of communal tension. I was left with no option but to walk back home. It could have been a happy moment for me as I could have spent the entire time watching birds and sky, but that day I decided to go home. Even the air felt heavier and quieter than usual that day. When I entered the fields, I saw some boys coming towards me. I could sense their mischievous looks even though I had not stared directly at them. I looked down and walked past them quietly as if I had not even seen them. I bit my lips nervously until I had crossed the big banyan tree, till then I had not dared to look back. I was nervous and felt uneasy in the chest,

I looked back to check...no, they were not following me. It gave a sigh of relief as I made myself comfortable on the small stone platform, which nearby farmers had made below this big and shady tree. It was here that they ate food and took a little nap in the sweaty summer afternoons...

But, today not a soul could be found here. I had heard from Baba that many Hindus were not going to their fields as they feared for their lives. Suddenly, I began to sweat when I realized that Baba had instructed me to use the village road for going to school, but I was completely lost in my thoughts and had taken this short-cut through the fields. I decided that it was foolish to rest here, when people were being killed ruthlessly and that too without any provocation. I sensed someone standing close to my head, I opened my eyes in shock ....those boys were back but now they were accompanied by three youths with wooden sticks in their hands and a dirty look in their eyes. "Thud" someone hit me from behind and then everything went black.

The only thing I could remember when I woke up the next day in my mother's lap was that someone had hit me on my head with a heavy metal and everything went dull and black after that. When I opened my eyes, I was at my home. The continuous sobs of my mother were the first sounds I heard. There was acute pain in my arms and slight numb feeling in my lower half. I tried to get up but I could not raise my head as my neck cramped with the stretching. I decided to give up. My eyes were the only things which were moving and still under my control. I had no courage left to talk to my parents and tears rolled down from my eyes as I tried to speak, but words refused to fall from my mouth.

A mother understands the unspoken words of her child; a mother understands what her child wants when he has not even developed any language. She knows when her child is thirsty, when he wants food or when he simply wants to be with his mother. So, I was assured that Bibi would understand what I wanted to say. I looked into her eyes, she understood that I was trying to speak; I wanted to tell something to Baba. She understood when I moved my finger towards the door, she called him, though never speaking his name, for it was forbidden for women to call their husband by name.

It was almost a week now and my injuries had healed to an extent; I was able to walk but not too freely. I was lucky that some farmers had spotted me; otherwise I would have been dead that day. Over the next few days, we heard that people were being killed, many people were thinking of leaving their ancestral homes and fleeing to Amritsar while some people still had faith that any such incident would not occur in our small village of Kot Qaisrani. The people who had attacked me that day were strangers, as I told Baba later when I regained my speech. I knew everyone in the village and I was sure that I was attacked by outsiders, but the question was who these people were and where they were hiding in the village. The village headman appealed to everyone to help in locating the culprits who had nearly killed me.

All the people who had gathered for the meeting stood up one by one, dusting their clothes with their hands as if trying to say that they had no idea about the culprits and all they cared was to save their children first. Baba too came back home, worried and tense. He had lost his faith in village headmen. He quietly opened the wooden door and moved slowly to the veranda throwing his weight on the wooden *charpoy* lying there. It creaked and stirred a little under his weight.

This was not his usual way to enter the house, on normal days, he would shout out, "*Bhagonwali*, where are you? Fetch

25

me a glass of Lassi quickly..." and then he would call out the names of his children one by one, "Rajje, Rani, Veena... where is everyone? Come, see what I have got for you to eat..." and the children would surround their dear Baba, although they never dared to hug or kiss him. I was very shy and Baba knew it very well. So, my share was passed to me quietly by my sisters who knew I would never ask for it myself.

But that day, everything was strange. Baba was not in his usual self, everybody was quiet as if they knew that something wrong was going to happen. That evening, we had a visitor, her name was Samina Bibi. She used to do sundry jobs in the houses like helping women with new-born babies or grinding wheat and spices occasionally. She was very poor and had no family; my mother called her whenever she was expecting some guests. Samina Bibi would be called two days before to grind the wheat into fine flour with the help of the hand-operated *chakki* made up of two huge circular stones with a wooden handle at one side. Samina Bibi was a very talkative lady; she had access to each and every house in the village and always had something interesting to share in her gossip. She was a kind of local reporter of the village. She was a cheerful lady, but that day her face was pale when she asked for Bibi. My youngest sister Veena took her inside the room. Within minutes Baba was also summoned inside the room. I sensed something wrong as I had never seen any woman talk to Baba behind closed doors and that too in the presence of my mother.

After about an hour Samina Bibi left our house while I was ordered to look after my sisters who were playing in the courtyard, I was also instructed to bolt the main door tightly. I saw Baba leaving the house in a hurry with a jute bag in his hand. My sisters were still playing outside, unaware or bothered about the situation. When I finally gathered courage to peep inside the room, I was shocked to see all the metal trunks lying open with clothes and sheets scattered everywhere. Bibi was holding a box of jewels and counting the coins in the box. She looked at my face but had no time to talk to me.

I stood there for a long time watching her stuffing everybody's clothes in a thick coarse bag, carefully wrapping up the jewelry in clothes. I realized that she was sobbing as she was madly running here and there with articles in her hand. I could not take this any longer, so I decided to ask her, "What is wrong, Bibi...Why are you packing up clothes?"

She said nothing but came closer to me and cupped my face in her hands. Now I could see that her eyes were moist. She hugged me tightly and we both wept. I understood what she could not say.

"Why? Why are we leaving? This is our house, our village, why do we have to leave this place?" I kept on repeating questions which would not find their answers and probably which no one could answer.

Nobody knows why innocent people are made to pay the price of callous decisions taken by governments of the day. That handful of people who were responsible for making us homeless, the situations which made our peaceful village into a battlefield, they had never even seen us, so how could they.....?

By late evening, Bibi was almost done with the packing work. By this time, my sisters had also come to know that we were leaving this place; yet they were hopeful of coming back as if it was some sort of trip which we occasionally had, when we went to my maternal uncle's place in Fatehabad. It was our annual trip around the *Rakhi* festival, when my mother would tie a golden thread on my uncle's arm and forcibly drop a piece of *ghevar* into his mouth. We enjoyed every part of it— the new clothes, sweets and sometimes even toys. But today, everyone was gloomy, as if we were going to some kind of exile-never to return.

Baba had returned home and was talking in whispers to Bibi. I looked at her face; she was nodding like an ever obedient wife. It was planned that she would go with the children and Baba would join her later at the station. We crept out of our house like thieves as the night approached. I could hear people talking and discussing the violence and killing which had become a part of our lives in the recent past. We had been instructed to bend low so that no one could see us leaving. I was carrying a heavy metal trunk on my shoulder followed by my younger brother Rajje, while my mother was carrying a big jute bag and holding the hand of Rani and Veena. Like one long human chain, we crept through the narrow lanes, hiding now and then whenever we heard someone's footsteps. We somehow managed to reach the station.

The train to Amritsar was ready to leave and had already whistled twice. We were relieved to see Baba waiting for us; he was standing on the footsteps of a sleeper coach and waving to us. It was a crowded place, full of immigrants who were running away to Amritsar to save their lives with their families. Metal trunks and luggage lying on the platform blocked our way. Everyone was in a hurry and no one was ready to cooperate. We pushed our way to the coach with great difficulty. Rani lost her doll while Veena was being punched and pulled from all directions.

We heaved a sigh of relief when we managed to set our foot into the coach. Baba was a strongly-built man and everybody had great regard for him in the village, but today he wore a timid look. Bibi managed to ask him in that chaos "Is everything ok? Why do you look so worried?"

"Our house, our house..... It has been set on fire!", He said pulling over the heavy metal trunk with one hand and wiping away his tears with his kurta's sleeve. "Bhanu just informed me....."

"What are you saying? It means that they were planning to burn us alive!" She said, grabbing his collar. "Yes, *Bhagonwali*, consider yourself lucky that you are still alive."

"Samina was totally right. She had heard those people. I would not have believed her but you had such faith in her. It is because of you that we are standing here alive..." Baba said grabbing her shoulders tightly.

I was stunned to hear what Baba had just said but there was no time to think about our house now, as we heard people on the platform were shouting. With a big push, the train had started to move as if forced by someone from the back. Some people with swords had reached the station and wanted to kill all the passengers. The train started to move slowly while people on the platform were being massacred and killed ruthlessly by swords. Some people even climbed on the train and started pulling out those standing near the gates. The shouts and swords continued while the train continued to move as if by some supernatural force.

Two men climbed into our coach and killed a man standing near the door, his son who was shocked .to see his father's blood and was thrown out of the moving train by the hooligans. Baba could not tolerate this, Bibi knew that he would indulge in a fight so she pleaded with him not to go; but it was too much for a man like him to bear atrocities. He grabbed hold of their swords with his bare hands and kicked them hard. One of them fainted and was thrown out of the train but the other one was not ready to give up, though his sword was snatched away by people he continued to thrash people, Baba suddenly plunged at him with great force and both of them fell out of the moving train still fighting.

Bibi shrieked in disbelief as she tried to rush to the door but she was pulled back by some women and the train door was quickly bolted from inside...

Chapter 4

LAHORE

The train kept crawling slowly and steadily as if nothing had happened. People lost their loved ones. Mothers were killed in front of their children, fathers and brothers were still missing, and infants were losing the laps of their mothers. Even those who had survived this onslaught of adversity, had boarded the train with trauma. A dubious fate was waiting for them at the other side of the border. The train was scheduled from Muzaffargarh to Lahore. The only respite for the people was the six Gurkha regiment soldiers who were ordered to escort the train till it reached safely at Lahore.

Bibi could not stop cursing her fate while I looked at her hopelessly... Baba was gone, so, I was the 'man' of the family, it was now my duty to ensure that my mother, sisters and brothers were safe. I was still a child; but a big responsibilty had befallen on me. I realized that I had been sitting with Bibi on the floor since we had left, in fact I was still holding her *dupatta* in my hands like a small boy who had lost his father and would not let go his mother out of his sight even for a moment. I stood up and wiped my eyes, with arms crossed around my chest. I moved to the area where men folk were standing and discussing matters among themselves. They looked at me with sympathy; after all sympathy was the only thing which they could offer me at that time... most of them were too terrified to talk, while some were angry and openly hurling abuses at leaders and their parties.

This kind of discussion was not new to my ears. As a student, I was aware of the political changes. I had also once seen the photographs of Gandhi, Nehru and Jinnah in a newspaper. Baba had told me that Congress and Muslim league had disagreed on various matters and partition was inevitable.

Little had we thought that one day we will be uprooted from our homes in the dead of night and we will have to flee like thieves. Everything was left behind- our home, cattle, fields...though I had seen Bibi packing up clothes and some jewelry in a bag but a big portion of the money and gold was hidden in the mud wall of the store room. She had full faith that one day we all will return to our home once these riots were over.

The train kept moving nonchalantly; it was evening when we came to know that the train was very near to the Lahore station. Suddenly with a big jolt the train came to a screeching halt; before we could look what had happened we heard people shouting and running towards the train with swords and lathis in their hands. They had gathered there to loot the train and abduct the women. People panicked and cried for help. It was at this time when the six Gurkha soldiers, who were escorting the train, emerged like heroes with their guns and fired six rounds. The attackers were not aware of this and many of them fled back to the fields from where they had emerged. Some of them who had entered the train were beaten to death by the people. The firing and battle of swords continued for the next thirty minutes in which two soldiers died but they did their job till the last breath of their life. So, with the help of brave soldiers and a united crowd of the train, the hooligans were defeated.

Many locals had gathered around the train by this time. They advised everybody to leave the train and walk towards Lahore by foot. They had heard that more loot and abduction was planned by some miscreants at the Lahore station, so it was better to leave the train.

The feeling of sheer brotherhood and humanism was there in the hearts of the people during such turbulent times. I could not understand how some people can be so good to strangers, while on the other hand their community members go on looting and murdering people. With great difficulty, we reached the Lahore DAV College. There, we met with the refugees who were going towards Amritsar. They had gathered there from different parts of Sindh and were waiting to board a train.

Here I met Harnam, a boy of my age. When he narrated his story of survival, I was shocked. His grandfather was killed in broad daylight in the streets of Mangtanwala... he was returning from his sweets' shop. He was an old, bearded man of the seventies. His body was thrown at their doorstep. Some people from *gurudwara* came and quietly took his body for last rites after midnight. Streets were dead silent. People had left their homes and were temporarily hiding at school yards, grain markets and other such locations.

33

Harnam described how he, along with his family members, had to jump the wall to get out of their home at midnight. Getting out of the main door was too unsafe as they had been hearing rumbling of trucks along with gun-fires; with great difficulty they had managed to reach the *Gurudwara*. There was a small room on the first floor of gurudwara which was used to store utensils for *langar*. The size of the utensils was big enough to conceal three children at a time. Many of his friends were pushed into these and covered up with gunny bags. Very little space was left for them to breathe properly. They were strictly instructed not to move if the door was forced open. Women were kept in a separate room. But, Harnam's mother and some other women had refused to leave their children alone. All these women lay huddled together in the corner of the room praying silently. In the dim lit room, only heartbeats and sobs were audible.

Men were guarding the Gurudwara with swords and sticks, some had guns but they were no match for an angry mob of thousand bigots who surrounded them from everywhere. They put up a brave fight, though very less in number...when the last men fell, only then the angry mob could enter the gates of Gurudwara. One by one all the locks were broken and doors fell apart. Harnam could hear shrill cries of women in the nearby room. He stood up. He knew his end was near. He wanted to hug his mother once last time. She was hardly visible in that dim lit corner. She knew her son was looking for her. She stood up and hugged him. They cried bitterly holding each other. Just then the door swung open. Two men tore away his mother from him and hit him hard on head. That was the last time he saw his mother alive. She was pleading with them to let her son go...she was carried away by two men.

The next morning Harnam could hardly open his eyes, his head pained and he could not breathe. He had to push away two bodies lying on him. When he gained some energy, he got up. His legs were shaking. He came downstairs. People had gathered at the small well nearby. Some policemen were taking out the swollen bodies from the well one by one which had now turned into a heap. He saw his mother's body lying near the heap. It was swollen and unrecognizable. He rushed towards her and pulled out his turban cloth and quickly covered her body...

* * *

Life at a refugee camp was not an easy one either; we were left with no option but to live in filthy conditions. Outside the refugee camp, dead bodies were lying here and there and nobody was ready to pick them up. Everybody was busy running for their own life. Next day a fresh batch of refugees arrived at the Lahore DAV College. I saw passengers crying with pain. One of the boys told me that he had not eaten anything for the last two days; out of the five hundred people who boarded the train, three hundred were killed outright. The whole train had absolutely no baggage as their entire luggage was looted. There were wounded people with bloodstained clothes; they were shivering with pain and wet clothes due to heavy rains, but none of them had any blankets or quilts. The monsoon was on its full swing and had been merciless as we heard that many roads were submerged, bridges collapsed and train tracks were washed away due to heavy rains. There was dirt, mud, blood stains and dead bodies of animals and human beings scattered all over the roadside. We ran into another trouble when Cholera broke out in the refugee camp making adults sick and killing infants almost every day.

Everywhere I saw people vomiting, children crying of unbearable abdominal pain. Someone told me that it was due to the poor sanitation and drinking of contaminated water.

Sick people were feeling more thirsty and consuming poor quality of water which further worsened their condition. Their frail bodies had been almost emptied by the watery diarrhea due to Cholera.

At this stage, when our possibilities of surviving were dim and even God seemed to be angry with us, it was the RSS which turned out to be our saviors.

Chapter 5

AMRITSAR

The RSS

Thousands of shattered families from all over Punjab and neighboring areas were coming to Lahore DAV College and its hostel. From here, they were being taken to trains escorted by Dogra and Gurkha soldiers to Amritsar Camp and further to Delhi. Indeed the most commendable services were that of RSS and soldiers who were risking their lives every day to rescue refugees who were still trapped.

During Partition, when Pt. Nehru was finding it difficult and feeling helpless in the midst of bloodshed, anarchy, loot and rape; it was the RSS that helped to organize over 3000 relief camps for the refugees who were migrating from West Punjab every day.

Nearly four hundred Muslim families were sheltered in the Lahore DAV college, while we the non-muslims, had to move out to the Amritsar camp. The rains were creating havoc and many buildings of *Shah Almi* and *Wichowali* areas of Lahore had collapsed, brutally killing a refugee family of eighteen people from Delhi. So, refugees could not think of living in these abandoned *havelis* anymore.

A small hospital was managed by RSS doctors and nurses who were working in Lahore medical college. Harnam observed that everyday few Swayamsevaks roamed around in jeeps escorted by Dogra soldiers to rescue the Hindu and Sikh families trapped in various localities. This was a risky work as Muslim police was not cooperating in spite of the fact that Pt. Nehru had visited the college camp and had assured that there will be no further slaughter and genocide.

Harnam told that two jeeps had left in the morning but only one jeep had returned in the evening; it had lost track and the only their escort vehicle carrying Dogra soldiers had returned??. Their fellow members of RSS were worried about their fate. Next day, a lone survivor of that batch managed to reach the college back safely. He narrated a harrowing tale that during evacuations they were separated from the escort vehicle, due to which they lost track. When they asked Muslim police to help them…they were beaten up by the police who turned hostile. All Swayamsevaks and the rescued families were taken to a secluded place and killed mercilessly. He had managed to escape as he had got down from the jeep just a few minutes ago to search the escort vehicle.

* * *

These two cities of Lahore and Amritsar had suffered more physical, economic and social damage than any other city during this chaos. The city of Amritsar was almost in ruins when we reached there. Like other cities, cholera had spread here too. Failure of electricity and water supply was making the situation worse. Sweepers and sanitation workers had been lured to jobs of drivers and coolies which were earlier a dominance of Muslim population.

We were living in a half torn canvas tent and were at the mercy of weather Gods. Every evening, Harnam and I jostled with others to get into the long line of refugees. We would wait for hours to see the trucks arriving with food packets. We had sisters and brothers to feed. We could never imagine going empty handed.

All the refugees coming from different parts of Punjab were indebted to RSS. When everyone despised them, only the RSS stood by them. They arranged for the safe passage of elderly, women and children in each and every *mohalla*. The *pracharaks* arranged for our food, clothing and medical help. They taught us some techniques in self-defence. When the entire Punjab was burning and political leaders in Delhi were sitting helplessly and shamelessly witnessing the bloodbath, it was the *Swayamsewaks* of RSS who reached the people first, helping them to find a safer place. They displayed sheer brotherhood and true humanity by risking their own life for total strangers. Not only they helped stranded Hindu and Sikh families, but also saved many Muslim families and led them to the Muslim league refugee camps. The RSS with its discipline, physical strength and true patriotism, was the real hero of partition.

Meanwhile, fresh batches of refugees were arriving regularly in the Amritsar camp. They narrated such spine chilling tales of murders in Lahore that we considered ourselves lucky. We had left Lahore at just the right time. One of the refugees told how the mass combing of Hindus had begun by some groups. They would sit on the roadside in a group of four or five people playing cards casually. Their weapons and knives were concealed a few feet beneath the ground where they were sitting and they concealed a small dagger in their *langots* in a way that even police could not find it while searching them. Whenever they saw someone coming down the street, they would approach that person offering him a smoke and inviting him to play cards. When the poor fellow revealed his religion they would brutally kill him in a cold blooded manner and again hide their bigger weapons beneath the ground and sit back to play again.

"Now they believe in quality and not quantity killing, my friend", the refugee said.

"How?" Harnam asked him.

"Now they are selectively killing important people of the Lahore city like the renowned professors, Bankers, Lawyers, journalists and other such people. Yesterday, they killed the Registrar of Punjab University. The innocent man was living just across the street from his office. He had just reached his office on foot after a hearty breakfast from his home across the street when five people wearing masks pinned him down in his office. Four people held his arms and legs and one of them pounced on him with an open dagger. Shouting their religious war cry, he slit the Registrar's throat like they killed the chicken making a half slit in the neck so that it can die on its own bleeding to death. The registrar was rushed to hospital but he bled to death on the way to hospital.

With each passing day, we were hearing such brutal stories. Humanity had died long ago. Now, there were only beasts, which cared for nobody. Even babies were not spared. One of the refugees told how he was badly injured when he saw a baby of two months crying bitterly. He tried to pacify him with a candy he was carrying but the baby still cried. Some hooligans with swords were following their group. It was ultimately decided to leave the baby then and there in the thick jungle as its cries would reveal their location. With a heavy heart the group moved forward. They heard the hooligans bouncing the baby in mid-air and cutting it down with their swords. As if it was a game; as if it was not a human baby, but some sort of ball, which they kicked and slit. No mercy. No shame. No heart.

I considered myself lucky that I was safe and now in an Indian city. Every day the refugees would go up to look into the registers, hoping against all odds that maybe their relatives were alive. I had given up hope of finding Baba again. However, Bibi was still adamant that he was not dead. "He might be injured badly, but he is certainly not dead", she would say dreamily staring in a direction.

One day, when I returned to the tent, I saw Bibi smiling with tears in her eyes. She was hugging a lady while a well-built man stood with them. He was Bibi's cousin from her maternal aunt as I came to know later. His name was Tek Chand, his wife was in an advanced stage of pregnancy. He was worried about her, he intended to reach Karnal soon where her relatives lived so that the delivery could be made in proper hands. He proposed that we should pack our belongings immediately and board the first train that was available. He had seen such atrocities meted out to people in the trains that he decided we should board a goods' train instead of a normal train.

We quickly packed our things. I bade goodbye to Harnam who was still at the Amritsar Camp for a few more days until destiny took him elsewhere. While climbing up the train, I had a hunch that this was not going to be a safe journey either.

Chapter 6

PHAGWARA

Though Bibi had protested against travelling on a goods' train with a pregnant lady, but my uncle thought it was better than dying here in an unknown place among strangers; moreover, he was informed that many of his wife's relatives had settled in Karnal. So, we were left with no option but to comply with his orders.

The train was moving at a modest speed, but we were feeling very cold. As all our bedding and clothes were looted, we all sat huddled close to each other in order to feel warm. We had hardly crossed Jalandhar station, when my maternal aunt Shanti Devi started having delivery pains. With great difficulty, my mother urged her to stay calm till the next station. So, when we reached Phagwara, we had no option but to get down from the train. My aunt was at the advanced stage of delivery and we had no source or vehicle to get her to the doctor.

The time was running out and we had to save the mother and the child. Initially, nobody came forward to help us, people were busy running here and there and looking for the trains which were arriving and leaving the platform. Everybody ran hither and thither. Bibi took charge of the situation at this crucial moment. She summoned all the children to fetch wooden sticks, my uncle was asked to fetch warm clothes and blankets for the mother and the child. I was summoned to look for wooden cots and rags so that she could cover up the place while delivery; seeing this few women came forward to help Bibi. The waiting rooms were too crowded and moreover, evacuating so many people with their luggage could have been an uphill task, apart from being time consuming.

Quickly, Bibi pointed towards a secluded area of the platform which was partly covered by long wild bushes. I managed to find a cot and rushed to Bibi; she smiled approvingly at me and waved me to go away. My sisters could get only a few torn pieces of clothes and some paper. They laid my aunt safely on the cot and one of the women ignited fire from the rags and torn paper to beat the cold morning. With rags and bushes, the place was covered and the women formed a circle around the cot. I saw my uncle running breathlessly towards them, he was carrying a blanket and a torn shawl in his hands. His face was white as snow and he was sweating profusely even in that cold weather. One of the women motioned him to stop. She took the shawl and blanket from him, she asked him to get warm water. My uncle ran back towards the exit while we heard a very faint crying voice of a new-born baby. My uncle had returned back with a hot kettle which he was holding carefully with one corner of his turban cloth. He was congratulated as both mother and baby were safe and he had become the father of a son. After several hours had passed, I saw Bibi coming out towards us. She was looking very exhausted; she had a faint smile on her lips but tears in her eyes.

She hugged me and my sisters and thanked us for showing so much courage. We were also informed that we had to stay for forty days in Phagwara as it was a custom that the newborn and the mother could not be moved to another place before that time. We all moved to an abandoned Mosque, where the mother and baby were given a corner along with a cot and some blankets. This was the only luxury which my Uncle could afford to give to his wife and his baby boy, whom he named 'Azaad' as he was born in a free country. He himself did some petty jobs to earn a modest meal for each of us. I offered to work but he strictly forbade me from moving outside the mosque in turbulent times. Instead, I was assigned to work as an errand boy for his wife and baby. Bibi cooked meals and fetched water; my sisters washed clothes and looked after the baby and my aunt, so each was assigned a specific task.

My uncle had forbidden me to do any work for money as he was concerned about my safety. People were still doubtful of each other. The deserted mosque in which we were living, was far better than the Phagwara refugee camp. I met many refugee boys of my age, while fetching some random things for my aunt and her newborn baby. One of them told how his newborn brother had succumbed to dysentery. There were at least a thousand people in the camp living under horrible conditions. They had no access to clean water to bath or to drink. People were dying of Cholera and Dysentery every day.

It was again the RSS Swayamsevaks, who were toiling day and night to help us refugees with whatever help they could. During the time of partition, there were two RSS camps underway in Punjab. One RSS camp was in Phagwara and other was in Sangrur. The Phagwara camp had nearly 1400

Swayamsevaks. Their camp activities were immediately ended the day, when partition was announced. Since then, these brave men had been evacuating people and ensuring their safety at the risk of their own lives.

The schools were suspended and turned into centers for distributing food and clothing to the arriving refugees.

Many local people came forward to help these centers. Every day, a fresh batch of chapattis was prepared by ladies for the trains arriving at the Phagwara station. Children and men would carry these chapattis to the station, and throw them to the refugees sitting on train tops as this was the only food, which was light to catch and could be easily thrown.

Strange is the nature of the human heart, it attaches itself to the people and thinks that they are going to stay together forever. We had grown so fond of baby Azaad that we didn't realize, it was almost time to part with him...

✧✧✧

Chapter 7

DELHI GROWS OUT
IN EVERY DIRECTION

After forty days were over since we had shifted to Karnal camp, which was near a canal. My aunt went to live with one of her relatives, while my uncle accompanied us. He was keen to settle Bibi and then only, he could return to his duty as a husband and a father. I really admired his sense of duty. Had it not been for him, I would have felt so lonely and terrible. We kept on moving from one camp to another. After Karnal, we shifted to Nisingh. Weather conditions were very bad here, and many people died. Somebody told us that land was being allocated in Delhi, so my Uncle decided that it was time to move to Delhi.

Beaten, hungry and tired, the refugees of our camp headed for Delhi knowing little that they will not be welcomed there. There was lots of resistance as local people

47

saw them as outsiders. The Hindu population of Delhi did not want these homeless and poor people to move into their posh neighborhood, while the Muslim population was fearful that these refugees who had been witness to massacre and killings, were seemingly looking for revenge. So, a bunch of residents of the old city met Mahatma Gandhi and Pandit Nehru. Together they decided that the refugees will be moved out of the old city and settled in newer areas. Thus began the expansion of Delhi in every direction. It was not an easy task and took a lot of time and effort. We had no place to go but wait in the temporary settlements in Delhi.

Old forts, deserted mosques and medieval structures were the temporary home for us. While residing in one of the temporary tents in an old haveli, we met with people from Lahore. One such family was that of Gurpreet singh. They were a very affluent people. The family owned horses, cattle, goats, chickens and even sheep. The children went to English school in Lahore, but for a brief period of time only, as the tension grew continuously. One night after getting a tip from a high official they packed their children, some cash and jewelry and headed for Amritsar in their jeep. Though it was very dark, yet they could see limbs of people lying around and bodies floating in canals. He was allotted a barren land in Punjab, in lieu of hundreds of acres left behind in his native village. The family which rode on cars and jeeps was now riding bullock carts and camels. They had degraded from riches to rags overnight.

Hearing such stories from people always left me weak but it also encouraged me to look forward to the future. If people like this could survive in such conditions, then what was our position in comparison to them?

Agricultural lands were acquired and cramped housing areas came up virtually overnight. Some of these were B.K.

Dutt colony, Ramesh Nagar, Malviya nagar, Tilak Nagar and Hari Nagar ashram.

Many Sindhis were also arriving on foot from Karachi and Umerkot. They were asked to settle in parts of Rajasthan,Gujarat, Maharashtra and Madhya Pradesh. Poor people having no papers with them, had to fight for decades to find a decent home and agricultural land. Refugees were building thatched huts in camps like Kingsway, Reeds line and even Khalsa College. A large Sikh population was shifted and settled to Inderpuri.

Land was acquired from the villagers of Khampur and Shadipur to settle the large population of Hindus and Sikhs together with people of NWFP. These areas came to be known as Patel Nagar and Rajinder Nagar. Many people settled down in Lajpat Nagar, Amar colony and Tilak Nagar. Rajouri Garden soon turned into a Punjabi locality. As Delhi began to swell up, the refugees were further shifted out to parts of Haryana, Rajasthan, Gujarat and even Maharashtra.

A minister was appointed for the rehabilitation of refugees and schemes were made to get them proper accommodation, schools and jobs. But, perhaps the most difficult task was to search for the missing people.

I went with my uncle to a big *maidan* where all the refugees would gather in the morning. Everyday people were called from various villages and land would be allotted to them based on their land holdings in Pakistan. It was our turn and I represented my Baba. We were allotted 3 acres of land at a place called Pinangwa which was a remote area of Mewat.

Mewat was known as a Muslim area and we were not very keen to move there. Many of the refugees had settled in Gurgaon city where work opportunities were still good. My

49

Uncle decided that I had some experience in farming so it was not a good idea to settle for a job. Moreover, I had still not completed my education. Bibi was too shattered to take any decision, so we were left with no option.

My uncle was eager to settle us in Mewat so that he could return to his wife whom he had not seen since a month. We were informed at the bus stand that Mewat roadways had only few buses, and the next available bus will come after three days and seats were already booked for it, so ours was put in the waiting category. My uncle could not wait for three more days, so all of us including Bibi made the journey in a truck which was going towards that area. When we reached Pinangwan, it was getting dark. The village wore a deserted look and the signs of loot and massacre were everywhere. While the cities were overflowing with the refugees looking for a suitable place to settle down with families, here in this remote area, we were free to choose any available house. Bibi walked up to a Pucca house and touched its door which was wide open, the courtyard had a big Neem tree and a well beneath it.

"This is going to be our house", she said in a trembling voice to my uncle. All of us were dead tired and hungry, but it was for the first time when I slept peacefully since the riots broke out.

Uncle made the necessary arrangements of acquiring the land, finding the tillers and sowing the crops of Jowar and Bajra. I went with him everywhere so that I could understand how to manage everything once he left. He stayed with us for fifteen days and when he was ensured that everyone was safe and fields could be managed properly, he left for Karnal.

Bibi's tears had never left her eyes since we left Pakistan but now she had to live alone in this strange new country which was "ours?" I tried to console her in every possible way and worked really hard day and night to make ends meet.

We were trying our best to adjust to the new climate and with new people, but everything went in vain. The local people looked at us with suspicion and the tillers demanded more money than they deserved. My youngest brother became very ill and my sister developed a strange eye disease due to which she could not see at night.

Bibi had been very quiet and still during this one year, watching everything silently, when one day she broke her silence.

"We have to get out of here; I will not let you die here", She said...

Chapter 8

MEWAT—THE HOME OF TABLIGHI JAMAAT

Living in Mewat for one year brought me in closer contact with the local Meos. They were originally landless cultivators as I came to know from the tillers of our land. They had something different in their customs, I could sense that they were different from the Muslims we had lived with in Dera Ghazi khan.

I had nothing much to do except looking after the fields. I had not much knowledge of crops, so I had no choice but to rely on the tillers. Some of them were young but I was particularly fond of Rahim Baba as everyone called him. He was of around sixty years, but was the most knowledgeable among them. I loved to sit and talk with him about the history of Mewat. Though Bibi would have forbidden me to do so, she was still afraid of anyone who came to our house.

53

He told me that Meos were originally cattle rearers like the Meenas of Rajasthan. They were converted to Islam during the period of Aurangzeb. Yet, they had not fully accepted its rituals. They had always followed dual customs.

"So my grandfather had both the *nikaah* and the *saat phere* ceremony, like Hindus when he got married", Rahim baba chuckled.

"How is it possible?"

"Yes, our forefathers were staunch believers of Lord Shiva. When Britishers came here, they were surprised to see that our cultures, traditions, even our clothes were not like Muslims of other regions. We wore dhoti kurta and did not know how to recite kalma."

"Then... who changed you?" I was curious.

"When Maulana Ilyas came to Mewat in 1920s, he was surprised to see the Muslims there. He immediately decided that they should be taught the basic principles and teachings of Islam. He set up Masjids here in a proper manner, which were earlier being used to store cattle fodder. Then he established Tablighi Jamaat in 1926 to educate people about Islam."

"So you changed yourself after that?"

"No, there was not much change in our traditions and we still carried on practices like Govardhan puja; but then partition changed everything", He said with deep pain in his eyes.

"Yes, it has changed everything", I couldn't agree more.

"You know that the Muslims of Malerkotla were protected by their Sikh neighbours at the time of partition, but here they were massacred in large numbers in the states of Alwar and

Bharatpur. There were lootings and bloodbaths in spite of the fact that we had been practicing dual religion since years, following both Hindu and Muslim traditions. Yet they killed thirty thousand Meos." Rahim baba was emotional now.

" But I still see a Muslim majority in this area..."I was still confused.

"Yes, during the time of partition and population exchange, many Meos had left this place and had reached the border of Rajasthan to go to Pakistan, but then Mahatma Gandhi came to know about this, and he himself came to the nearby village of Ghasera."

"So, you saw him?"

"Yes, I saw him for the first and last time in my life. He summoned the village headmen at the temple well. Everybody gathered there, he announced that there was no need to leave Hindustan and that all the Meos who had left, should immediately be called back from the Rajasthan border. Many Meos were temporarily camping in some parts of the Gurgaon district, they also came back after the violence subsided."

"But top political leaders never came to help us, or said anything to Jinnah so that we could pass the border safely without so much trauma and suffering."I had so many questions in my mind. Why were *we* left to the mercy of fate then?

"Partition changed the Meos forever" Rahim baba said, resuming his talk again.

"When the Meos were killed in Alwar and Bharatpur, they thought that it was some kind of punishment which Allah had given them because they had not followed Islam properly. After that, they decided that it was better for them to stay at one side of religion. They started growing a beard and wearing skull caps. Tablighi Jamaat further paid them wages and induced them to learn namaz and memorize verses from Quran. Meo children were sent to Delhi to receive education from Jamaat. They returned here and started preaching Islam in all parts of Mewat".

I was lost in thought when Rahim Baba gently touched my shoulders.

"I will give you a piece of advice if you trust me...", he said looking into my eyes directly.

I recognized this gaze. It was that of truth. I had seen a similar look in the eyes of Samina Bibi when she came to our house to warn us. That look of emergency which foretells that something bad is going to happen soon. That look of pain because the listener does not trust you, however you must play your part of warning them.

"Yes Baba, what do you want to say ?"

"Leave this place with your family... immediately, the tillers are not to be trusted. They are planning to demand an increase in wages and if you resist, they will cut down your family in one go", Rahim Baba said looking in the direction of tillers who were engaged in their work.

"You are just a kid, even if your uncle has set up everything... yet you are an outsider here. No one will care where you or your family has vanished overnight."

"Don't worry about the land as long as you have papers, you are the legal owner. Your uncle has a friend here in *Panchayat* who will take care that your land doesn't get encroached." Rahim baba said imploringly.

Run... leave... save your family

Bibi was right. We could surely die here...

Chapter 9

GURGAON

Yes, that is the best thing to do if we really want to live. I am sure that one of us will succumb to the harsh climate of this place' I told Bibi not revealing her the truth. 'Now when Baba is no more with us, it is my responsibility to look after my family and ensure that no one dies.'

I asked my sister to pack up all the things as we were moving from this wretched place. Bibi was still not in a position to react fully to what was happening around her. Her left eye was sore and constantly wore water as she cried day and night. She had developed insomnia and cursed the hooligans who had pushed Baba out of the moving train.

We left the house and went to the bus stand, nobody uttered a single word. We had no one to inform that we were leaving. People were least bothered about our leaving the village. I was dying to receive a friendly smile and a brotherly embrace but all these things seemed to be a distant dream. In this kind of atmosphere where people were suspicious, brutal and selfish, all that I could get was an inquisitive look which demanded my details whether I was a friend or a foe, but not the least amount of sympathy.

Things began to look a bit hopeful when we boarded the bus to Gurgaon. Though it was like a normal journey, but I had this strong intuition that our period of trials was going to be over soon. I looked around to study people on the bus; everybody was staring at some invisible point. While children chatted and ladies gave a glum and sympathetic look, men were quiet. On any other occasion it would have appeared a very boring journey to me, but today even this silence was some sort of gift. After the scenes of massacre, bloody and spoiled clothes and that feeling of helplessness, which I had encountered all the way from Pakistan, was ironically a better journey for me and my family. Bibi was still lost in thoughts but her words still echoed in my ears "we must move out of here" as if God was speaking through her and He wanted us to move to a better place where we could hope for a better future.

It was not a very long journey, only a couple of hours. We got down from the bus at the Gurgaon bus stand. It was like a new world to me, I was observing things and people for the first time since we left Pakistan. Those few months spent in Mewat were like a distant dream where I was too busy in solving petty issues with the land tillers and had no time to think or reflect on how people walked or behaved.

My heart told me that something good was finally waiting for my family. We moved to the refugee camp set up by the local administrative bodies. I could not recognize anybody there, but surprisingly, I saw Bibi talking to a lady. I was stunned to see her this way. After all, she had remained nonchalant for the entire twelve months of our stay in Mewat.

Things began to settle and we were allotted a small lodging with the help of that lady—whom we began to call Bimla *mausi* soon after. Her husband had luckily survived and he promised to help us find Baba. I was glad that finally Bibi had a company and she was finally looking up to life. She was excellent in needle work and with the help of Bimla *mausi* she started a part time job. My sisters also assisted her in her work.

Tola Ram was Bimla mausi's husband who worked somewhere in Delhi, my mother had still not lost hope to find Baba, so one day she asked Tola Ram to accompany her to the refugee camps in Delhi. Though she had then come out of her traumatic condition, I could not encourage her to travel on her own, so both of us asked uncle Tola Ram to guide us to the refugee camp.

When we reached Delhi, he got down at a place called Delhi Cantt as he had to meet someone in the 'food corporation'. Bibi told him that we would not leave without him as she feared that we would be lost again. So, we decided to go with him and wait till his work was done.

It was a beautiful place with greenery everywhere. I could see several army trucks with soldiers in their smart uniforms with long rifles. Uncle Tola Ram was taking a lot of time and we were not allowed inside, so we sat on the platform erected on the opposite road facing the building gate. Bibi put a long veil on her forehead with her *dupatta* as it was getting hot. We were feeling very thirsty and so I decided that we should request them to allow us to drink some water from the tap which was inside the building compound. I reached the gate and knocked very slowly. I heard a familiar voice, "Who is there?"

I must be mistaken, but my heart said it was him. I knocked the gate again for the second time. This time nobody spoke, I was frightened for a second when the gate flew open suddenly. I move a few steps back, scared. It was Baba, in the uniform of a security man. He had a big scar on his face and was looking very pale.

We hugged each other, I held back my tears for several minutes. Baba too was in same condition. These were the tears which I had been holding back since I lost him in the train and converted myself to the 'man' while the fact was that I was still a young boy who simply adored his Baba. We stood there embracing each other for a long time without uttering a word when I heard a shrill cry.

Bibi had recognized him from across the road and came running towards him stopping just a few steps before. It seemed like she had lost her energy and her legs could not carry her forward any more. She fell on her knees raising her arms towards Baba.

This sudden excitement was too much for her to bear and she became unconscious. Baba could not believe his eyes and ran towards her to support her. He rested her head in his lap caressing her like a child. "*Bhagonwali, Bhagonwali* ye..."

It was like a new birth for all of us. I had given up all hopes to see my Baba again but today he was standing before my eyes, all flesh and blood with a big scar across his face.

My sisters were overjoyed to meet Baba, our neighbors praised Bibi's fate that she was lucky enough to get back her husband after all that massacre and bloodbath. Everybody praised God that He had shown mercy on our family. I had thanked God for the first time in the past six months. I had turned almost an atheist after we left Pakistan. Though, I had neither been a fanatica as well. Our family followed the principles of Arya Samaj, so I had hardly been to any temple or Gurudwara in Pakistan.

Now that Baba had returned home and he had a regular job in Delhi, he decided that all his children should be educated properly. So, all of us including my sisters got admission in a Government-run schools and our education was resumed.

Schools here in Hindustan were quite different from the ones we studied in Pakistan. This was a big school with a cement building and we had nice airy classrooms with wooden seats and benches, which was not the case in my school in Kot Qaisrani, where we used to sit out in the open and had only four rooms. These four rooms were seldom used as they were not properly ventilated and dark even during the broad daylight. Many of my teachers were Muslims and the teaching staff comprised only male teachers; while here we had few female teachers along with the males. Most of the teachers here spoke Hindi and were Hindus from upper caste. My classmates were mostly refugees and some local boys but we had no Muslim boy in our class. Back in Pakistan, I had many Muslim friends and many had actually helped our family in moving out safely from troubled areas, but the atmosphere of mutual understanding and brotherhood between the two communities was not the same now. I hated this feeling of suspicion, it was like living in a herd where each one of your community was welcome but any outsider was strictly prohibited. The Hindus, Muslims and Sikhs had lost their friendship forever.

My sisters were admitted to Vedic Kanya School, which had an all-female staff. They studied Home Science and Sanskrit besides the other subjects. It was like a luxury for them as most of their friends were either married off or stayed at home to do household chores. Baba respected women and had always believed in the equal rights for them. This was something which was quite unusual in those times and something which I inherited from him.

61

Peace had finally found its way to our new home in a new country which was full of people and hopes. Each one of us came here with a hope and it was now in our hands to shape up our future. Being the eldest of all, I had the moral duty of setting up a good example for my siblings to follow. Everybody worked hard—men, women, children even the elderly. We had no choice either. People had to forget their past and work with hands to fetch two square meals for their families. Sometimes during the night when the whole family gathered for meals, Baba would fondly recall his days in Pakistan. Though he was not a *pehelwan*, yet his diet was equivalent to the one. There was plenty of milk from our herd of cows but here we had no cattle. There was hardly any space, it was just a small room with a big wooden cot and a mat which was spread out during night to accommodate Bibi and my sisters for a sleep. While Baba slept on the cot with my younger brother, I had chosen a corner of the room to make myself comfortable, where I would often sit spending the entire night reading and re-reading my books. When Bibi would get up around 4O'clock she would gently cover me up with her worn-out shawl.

Those were very testing times for everyone in the family. My heart ached with pain, when I looked at my parents and siblings. We had a big spacious house with separate area for cattle, but here we had just a small room with a tiny backyard. We never knew what was hunger and hard work until partition befell on us. Eating habits were changed due to circumstances and we were thankful even if we got two meals in a day. Back in Pakistan our house was full of grains, ghee and pulses. How can I forget the ghee-laden *roti* which Bibi prepared on *tandoor*. Sometimes we would enjoy the *roti* made on *sanjhachulha*. All the *mausi's, maami's* and *Bhabhi's* of neighbourhood would gather and cook on a common *tandoor*. It was a social networking place of that time. Children played around, while women discussed their family life. We would not only share the *rotis* but also other eatables like *daal, sukhisabzi, ghee,* butter etc. *Lassi* was avoided at night and was limited to mornings and afternoons. Soon our tummies were full, but still Bibi would force us to drink warm milk which was boiled along with *mishri* and *elaichi*. On special occasions, we were treated with *patisa* and *malpura*. We enjoyed the days when a guest was expected. On these occasions, some part of the outer compound was dug up to fix wood and a big metal pot was adjusted carefully on it. We had vegetarian or non-vegetarian feasts depending on the taste of the visitor. A non-vegetarian meal needed overnight cooking so that the texture of meat and vegetables like turnip could be consistent. Bibi would also use special *masala* which was carefully grinded on a *silbatta*... onions, garlic, ginger, cloves, cardamom, pepper, nutmeg, cashew paste, cream...we kept on counting the ingredients which went into making the perfect curry. It was customary to feed the guests first. We could hardly wait, but I was the favorite child of my mother so a small bowl was secretly passed on to me...stealthily... and off I went with my prize.

Life was hard now and food choice wasn't much for us here. In spite of that, I was happy... at least trying to be...

Most of my classmates had either lost their father or their sisters and brothers in the massacre. I considered myself lucky that I was still with my family and finding Baba again was nothing less than a miracle.

Partition had snatched away all our comforts and material possessions but we were still together as one. We had still retained the dignity of our family, without money though... and it was this pride which I vowed to bring back to my family...

✧✧✧

Chapter 10

ALWAR

MY FIRST JOB

The year of 1952 was quite difficult and though I and my family had a series of problems to face, I was able to complete class X in this year.

When I escaped from Pakistan and finally settled in Gurgaon after moving from Mewat, I had hardly any decent clothes to hide myself. I had no warm clothes to wear and went to school with chattering teeth, and braving the harsh cold winters in my worn out shirt. For consecutive four years, my family could not afford to have warm clothes for the winters.

I had only two shirts—one was for wearing at the school and other was kept for home. Besides limited clothes, we had very little to eat. Ration was given at the refugee camps and people stood in long queues—men, women, children fighting and falling on each other to collect the small amount of sugar, rice, wheat and oil.

The really painful scene was when one day I saw Bibi standing in the line. She was sweating profusely and was not looking well, suddenly somebody shouted that wheat was short in supply and only few people could get it. People panicked and broke the queue, Bibi fell down and was almost trampled by the mob.

I ran towards her and pushed away two -three people who had fallen on top of her. She was unconscious and could hardly breathe. I took her to a safe place and promised her that she would never face a ration shop again. That day I decided that my family will rise above such poverty and my mother who had once lived a luxurious life, will not bear such extremity. Through the dint of hard work, I promised myself that I will create a better and comfortable future for my family.

Life is certainly not easy but for people like me, it was more than that. I wanted my life not just to be easy but very, very comfortable and affluent. My childhood life in Pakistan served as a benchmark for me, as I worked hard day and night to fight against the atrocities of life. I wanted to use education as a tool to rise above my peers, who had succumbed to petty jobs and sundry business to make ends meet.

I thought myself to be lucky as Baba supported the family while I cleared one exam after another. Victory could not hide itself from me and very soon I was awarded my first job —as a rent collector in Palwal district.

I often stayed at my office whenever I was late, but most of the days I left at the dawn and returned back at midnight. It was quite a tough and exhausting job. The Government had fixed one rupee as rent to be collected from each mud hut which was allotted to the refugees, somedays no one came while some days they had groups and groups of people who would stand in the small office waiting for their turn, there were rarely any defaulters so I hardly went out of the office. I continued my job as a rent collector for one year, but I wanted something bigger and preferably a more respectful position.

My dreams finally came true when one day I received an interview letter. I had cleared the central excise exam for which I had appeared a few months back. The venue for the interview was the Talkatora barracks near the Parliament house and I had to appear at 10 O'clock on the next day. After a round of formal introduction I was asked a few questions about freedom fighters of India, which I easily answered as General Knowledge had been my favorite subject. The result was announced later that week and I received a joining letter soon after.

Bibi was on cloud nine as she ran breathlessly in the street calling all her friends to have a look at the 'letter' which said that her son was now a '*Sarkari Babu*' or Government employee!

With moist eyes, I hugged her, she could not stop herself from rejoicing. It was a very big achievement for our family as no one in the neighborhood or our community had completed their studies or got a good job after partition. I became a trendsetter overnight, a real hero of the refugee community.

For myself, it was a moment to cherish, the first taste of hardearned happiness; yes, it was the first ray of happiness in our life since that fateful day when we left our dear home. It was the darkest night of my life, nobody knew if we will be alive next moment or not and then, a long journey, an alien land and unknown faces…those had been hard times.

"What are you thinking beta?...Those times are over now, God has been so kind to us..." Bibi could almost read my mind like a mother who always understands what her child wants even before he has learnt to speak.

I got posted as an excise inspector in the district of Alwar in Rajasthan. It was quite far away from Gurgaon so I had to stay there; it was not possible to commute every other day. This was the first time when I was separated from my family for such a long period.

Life in Alwar was full of experiences for me, but I had never shied away from doing any kind of work. The rented house was shared by four other colleagues who were of the same age, so it was a carefree bachelor life. Each one of us had divided the household chores among ourselves which were shifted every month, so that each of us could learn to cook, clean and wash.

Our room was near the railway station which was a big nuisance for me as I could not sleep during the night. I wondered how my roommates could manage to sleep in such a noise. Every night I would count the number of trains, I even learned their time table. I tried to convince my friends that they could shift to a better place, but they argued that they would not be able to find such a big house at the rent of Rs.10 per month elsewhere in the town.

Our office was not far away from our rented house, so every morning we had a good stroll till the office; we teased each other and cracked jokes on their way to the office. Some days we would take a Tonga just to have some fun while riding; now even the *Tongawallah* became familiar with us and he would offer to give us free rides but I always took care to pay him his due amount. After facing adversities in life, I had realized the power and necessity of money in one's life.

It was a carefree life and full of hopes for each one of us as we looked forward to getting married sooner or later.

It was June, the hottest month in North India when my marriage was fixed up by Baba. Nobody had seen the girl, not even Bibi. Her father used to commute with Baba every day on the same local train. So, the two friends decided one day that they will marry their children and seal this friendship forever. It was against the culture that would-be bride and groom should meet each other before marriage so I had not seen Meera before. The day was fixed and the marriage procession went on the camel back to the bride's place, though it was in the same city and not very far off but everybody wanted to bring back the customs they had seen and followed in Pakistan.

It was a very simple marriage with no pomp and show as Baba was strictly against such show-off which may cause burden to his 'friend'.

My life turned a new chapter in the form of a loving wife and a dutiful daughter in law-Meera. It was sheer luck that I got posted in Gurgaon from Alwar in the same year. Now, I could live happily with my newly- wedded wife and my parents.

Meera was a girl with plain looks. She hardly wore any make up or ornaments; she believed in real hard work and soon took the responsibility of the family. In the coming years, all my siblings were married and well settled. Meera was an excellent housekeeper who not only looked after my children but also helped to earn some money by her deftness in stitching and sewing jobs, which she took as a part time job.

But, was Bibi satisfied? No, like any other mother she had wished for a fair daughter-in-law for her fair and smart son, but Meera had a dusky complexion, not that she ever complained verbally about it but somewhere she was worried about the 'colour' of her would be grand-children.

But good deeds overcame the simple looks and soon Meera became her favourite. Bhaganwali had always praised the deftness of her daughter-in-law's work and now she admitted it openly even to her daughters that if they really want to become a good housewife, then they should learn it from Meera.

It was the beginning of a new chapter in life of Sukhdev as well. He was full of enthusiasm and energy to achieve 'something' in life but what was this 'something' and how it could bring back the lost glory of his life—this was still a riddle to which he had not found any answer yet...

Part–II

Chapter 1

MEERA

I was fourteen years' old when Baba proposed my marriage to his friend Balraj Dass's son. They had been commuting through the same train for almost five years. Baba worked in a bicycle factory in Delhi while Balraj dass was posted as guard in Army Cantonment area. Every evening, when *Baba* reached back home with his jute bag, I would run to fetch him a glass of water. Next, I would slowly take the bag from his left arm. His right arm was injured during the partition and had never healed.

One day when Baba came back, he asked me to make tea for him. I was surprised. Baba only preferred tea made by my Amma (mother). I went quietly into the kitchen. He was talking in whispers. I could hear words like "Marriage", "Meera". I concluded that they were talking about my marriage.

My elder brothers were serving in the army and had settled with their wives. My elder sister had been married just two years before, now I and my younger brother Sarjan were left in the house.

Soon that day came when I was married to Sukhdev. It was a simple affair. No pomp and show. I learnt that my Father-in-law did not want to burden us. I was grateful to him. With a heavy heart, my Maa bid farewell to her favourite daughter. I was worried not for my future or my husband, but for my Maa. Sarjan was planning to go to the Sainik School like my elder brothers so that he too could join the Army or Air force. Maa had an ailing body. She was not capable of cooking, cleaning and other household chores.

* * *

My mother-in-law welcomed me with open arms. I was stunned by her fair complexion and towering height. She was an absolutely right match for her husband. But I was not. I had always been taunted by my friends because of my dusky complexion. In spite of that, I had stayed away from any kind of makeup. I was worried that Sukhdev would find me too plain for him.

We just went on talking on our first night. I didn't realize when I dozed off. He was very understanding and mature, more like a friend. He wanted to know so much about me. He was also curious to share everything about himself. I thanked my stars. I had found the gem of a person as my husband. Next day, I went to my father's house as was customary for the newly wedded daughter after marriage. Everyone praised my luck. Sukhdev was very handsome and had a fair complexion, quite opposite to me, I should say. My ailing mother taught me a very important lesson of life that day, "Let everyone know your true beauty, let your work speak up for itself". I realized that there was no alternative to hard work, if I had to keep the house running.

Days passed into months. Sukhdev was frequently called to Alwar. He went back after spending 15 days with me. I realized that it was indeed a very small house. The mud courtyard made the floor dusty all day so I swiped and broomed the house twice a day. Everyone called my Mother-in-law 'Bibi' so I too called her "Bibi". She was a very hard working woman. Everyday she would get up at the crack of dawn. Though she never asked me to follow her rituals, I thought it was worthwhile.

So I followed her routine. Soon I started helping her in daily chores. I had learnt some needlework before. Now, she taught me how to draw more intricate patterns. She also came to know that I had studied till fifth grade only. She felt very bad for me. She had taken care that all of her daughters had at least completed high school. My youngest sister-in-law was studying even after her marriage.

I too wanted to study but due to my first pregnancy, I had to drop that idea. Days passed into months. Bibi and I became 'needle' buddies, chatting over every topic while completing our patch work. These patches were then sewed into white shirts. These shirts were then exported to various countries. That was the only information I cared about. What excited me more was the money I could save and how many pieces I could complete in two days. After every two days. Bimla *Mausi* would come to collect the sewed pieces, count them and give us money accordingly.

Though I had not completed my education, I maintained the daily accounts nicely. Bibi was impressed when I found out that we had been paid less. I had even kept a written record of that. Bibi also praised me for my cooking and deftness in keeping the house clean. Over the years my father-in-law had built two small rooms; the third one was being used as a store room, yet I tried to maintain its cleanliness as much as possible.

Almost four years had passed and I had become the mother of two beautiful daughters. Sukhdev had once revealed that Bibi was worried about the complexion of her grandchildren as I was dusky. Thankfully, she never complained about my complexion to me. Now, it was time for my brother-in-law to get married. With great excitement I had prepared everything for his wedding. Bibi was very happy, but she was no longer that energetic as she had been. I saw her wearing a worried look. I also saw her discussing something animatedly with Baba.

That helpless look on Baba's face was something new for all of us. He was a strong man but he also took to heart if Bibi said anything to him. Rajje and his newly wedded wife had to be accommodated. Bibi insisted that she and Baba would move to the store room, but I was adamant. It was poorly lit and segregated in a corner of the courtyard. I decided that I would move to it with my daughters. As Sukhdev visited us only once a month, so we could accommodate ourselves nicely.

After some cleaning and painting, the room started looking habitable. However, Bibi was still upset. Rajje's wife was finding it tough to adjust into our little home.

Chapter 2

BHAGONWALI

For Sukhdev, education had always been a tool with which he could overcome all his sufferings. As a young student, he had always been told by his teachers that education was the only treasure which none could snatch from you. By utilizing this treasure of knowledge, Sukhdev had marked a path for himself; on which he had to walk alone, as the torch-bearer for his entire family. I was very proud of my son.

He was a very hard-working man and never shied away from extra work. He was transferred from one city to another because of his reputation as a tough and a hard-working official who would not mind going to the homes of people for sorting out their problems and staying up late at night to complete the projects of the state and central government. He was immensely liked by the people and his work colleagues. He was soft spoken, never raised his voice, even in front of most irritating situations, or people.

I knew I was blessed with a dutiful child as a daughter-in-law. I was fond of Meera. Perhaps Rajje and his wife did not like it. I could not see my children fighting over petty issues. It was time they were separated to maintain peace and love within the family.

There were very high chances of Sukhdev being posted back to Delhi or Gurgaon,as he had told his Baba during his last visit. He had made a lot of savings also. I thought it was the best time to take a decision. I consulted my husband. He was heartbroken, ashamed. How could he ask his son to move out?

It was Sukhdev's second visit to home this month and he was fondly talking to Meera and asking her if the new bride that is; his younger brother's wife, had adjusted well in the family. Before she could reply, I entered their room. Meera retreated a few steps.

"Bibi, what happened, why are you up so late? Are you ok?" Sukhdev asked me imploringly.

"Yes, I am ok, you don't worry about me...actually I came here to discuss something with you son."

"What is it? Is everything going well in the house?" he turned towards Meera now.

"Don't look at her, I have not come here to complain about her, she is a gem, but a gem needs not be sacrificed in looking after the entire family. I know she is burdened with house chores, but she will never speak."

"Then what is it? Sukhdev looked puzzled.

"My son, I want you to find a new place for your family, now that your brother is also married and we have only two rooms. How will everybody adjust in this small house? Please don't think that I am throwing your family away but even your Baba wants the same thing." I managed to blurt out somehow.

Sukhdev knew that his Baba would never ask him to leave his house as he was a proud man and admitting in front of his son that he could not manage to adjust both his sons together in a small house was a touching matter, maybe that's why he had assigned me to talk about it.

No time was wasted in further discussions and Sukhdev bought a plot in a nearby area with the help of his brother-in-law who had just returned home on vacations. Sarjan lal was the youngest and closest brother of Meera, he had recently joined the Indian air force, and he was still unmarried. Meera, being his elder sister, wished him to settle soon but her mother fell seriously ill. There was nobody in the family to take care of the old lady as her elder sons were in the army and posted in different states so Meera decided to stay with her mother along with her family till she became well, and meanwhile Sarjan was given the responsibility to construct the house as Sukhdev could not stay for long.

"I never thought that one day I will leave this house in this manner", Meera said hugging me.

It was a rare sight between a mother-in-law and her daughter-in-law. All the neighbours had gathered together to bid farewell to Meera and her family. Though the house was still under construction, Meera had to stay with her parents and look after her ailing mother. I promised to visit her regularly at her mother's place.

MEERA

Days slipped into months and soon the time came when Sarjan had to leave to report back to his training in the Indian Air Force. The house was yet unfinished. My mother was still recovering. I wanted to save my mother at any cost; I hardly found any time to look after my children, so only Veera managed to pass in her exams. Preeto had failed. Thankfully Gyan my new born son was still away from school.

Those were the testing times. I had no option, but to act strong. I wanted to save my seriously ailing mother and look after the unconstructed house. I could not call Sukhdev to share my hardships. I took up the embroidery work to earn some extra income. With it, I could meet the expenses which the new house was demanding.

"I cannot see you suffering like this," said Sukhdev on his visit to home. This was his second visit within a month— something which he had not done in previous postings.

"Please don't come in such a small interval. I am ok and I am happy with the money you send to us." I replied.

"But why; I know you are all alone with all these responsibilities, I will talk to Baba, he can look after the construction of the house, you need not run from pillar to post to do sundry jobs like this" Sukhdev exclaimed in a low voice.

I looked at his face, it had grown pale.

"What a shame I have given to my family...my wife has to live with her parents, do petty jobs, look after the construction labours... No, my family deserves more comfort and this is my duty to look after everyone...not yours" He almost broke into tears.

"No, no why are you cursing yourself like this? how much sacrifice did you make by staying away from your family, by working hard day and night so that you are promoted to a good rank...I know very well."

I managed to pacify him. I assured him that I was not alone though Baba had little strength left. My own father and his closest friend had died long ago. Baba had become too weak, yet he visited our house to have a check at the construction work. Bibi was a constant support to me. She visited her grandchildren regularly. The only thing which bothered me was that I was not able to look after the study routine of Veera and Preeto. The girls were doing their work mostly on their own; getting up early and going to school, all by themselves.

"Don't worry, for that you can ask Veera to help you, she is a very matured and a responsible girl. I know she will understand your problem and help her sister in every possible way" Sukhdev assured me.

One day my mother died peacefully in her sleep.

Soon the days of hardships were over and our new house was ready for its masters the children were especially overjoyed, though it was not a very big house but it had a spacious bedroom, a living room, kitchen, a small room for children and a small courtyard, where they could sit and play and sleep at night during the hot summer nights. The girls were delighted by the kitchen with slabs and a basin for washing utensils. Till now, they had been working on a '*mudchulha*' and there was no separate area for the kitchen at their grandfather's home. They had to bundle up in a single room together and there was no space to accommodate any guest. Now they had a nice living room with a big glass show-case. Veera decided that she will decorate the house in the most elegant manner. Now she did not need to make any excuses to keep her friends away.

"We will put up lace curtains in the living room and thick dark curtains in the bedroom" Veera proposed.

"Yes, but we will have to save a bit dear, to buy curtains, as you see your younger brother and sister also need to be sent to school this year. Your father plans to rent out the first floor room to a tenant so that we are not left alone. We can also earn some extra money" I explained.

"I know mother, but why Pitaji wants us to save so much? Aren't we now well off?" Veera was still confused.

"Yes, my child, your father earns well. With my part time embroidery work we can afford good things. But we want to save more. We need to educate you and then get you married…" I sighed.

Getting her daughter married is a very sensitive issue for any mother, but for me it was like cutting off my right-hand. Veera was my emotional and physical support. It was Veera only who helped me in household chores, not only she was a brilliant student but also a responsible and caring elder sister. She earnestly taught Preeto due to which she was able to make up for the lost year and also scored well in her exams. I was too busy in house chores to attend their school and Sukhdev was posted far off, so Veera attended to the needs of her younger brother and sister. Veera was like a mother to them.

* * *

It had been seven years since we shifted to our new home; Sukhdev was finally promoted and transferred to Delhi airport, where he started working as a custom officer. Our children had grown up. Veera was doing her post-graduation. I had been receiving several marriage proposals for both Veera and Preeto, but I still could not make up my mind.

I knew that this was the right age for her to get married, but somehow I was too afraid to let my dear daughter go away like this. Bibi understood my situation. She was the first one to console me for my unknown worries.

"Why are you so worried dear?", Bibi asked me one day.

"No, I am just thinking how alone I will become after she leaves home I think I am too much dependent on her for everything; she is so responsible, so perfect in everything that I don't have to supervise anything, I am just free to do anything or go anywhere...", I replied.

"Yes, it is human nature to cling to those things which are not ours and daughters are like this only; you never know when they grow up and they are ready to leave your house."

"But, Bibi I don't understand this custom, we bring up our girls with so much love and one day they just leave us... or rather I should say, they have to leave us and live with strangers, whom they have never met in their life; why a child is snatched away from her mother like this...this breaks my heart" I said, wiping my tears.

"Dear daughter, why do you cry? Have you forgotten that once you were also in the same position? Didn't you leave your mother's house? Weren't you dear to your mother?"

"Yes, Bibi, I was...I was...but how will she adapt herself with new people, in a new house? I was not ready to give up."

"Meera, do not forget that God has given this power only to women; only she has the power to bring together two families and become a mother, a daughter, a wife. Only we, the women can play so many roles with perfection and don't forget our Veera is an educated girl. You had hardly studied till fifth standard, and you were just fourteen years' old when you were married but Veera is fully matured. She has the capability to handle things more easily than you or me." Bibi explained feeling proud of her granddaughter.

"Yes, I agree with you on all the things that you just said, but I know, I will never be able to make up for the loss when Veera gets married", I sighed.

"Don't worry, we will find a good family for her. Have you talked to Sukhdev about this? What is his opinion?", Bibi enquired.

"He cannot make up his mind, though he says that we should get her married in time so that her younger sister should not suffer; after all there is not much age gap between them. Preeto does not want to study further." I was finally composed now.

"Ok, then I will pray to God that my granddaughter gets married soon..." Bibi stopped herself from saying another word. She saw Veera entering the room; she was carrying her books in one hand and a jute bag in another.

Chapter 4

VEERA

It had been almost thirty three years now when we shifted to 'our' home… Pitaji had established himself well, all his children were married and living peacefully with their families. He was now a proud grandfather of two kids from his only son Gyan. He had retired long from his job and was now established as a consultant.

Though life and age had taken its toll on his body, (he had a minor heart attack), but, nothing could dampen his spirits and willpower. He was still full of love and emotions for every member of his family, like a protective patriarch.

For Amma, the marriage of her daughters had been a painful episode. She had not fully recovered from her migraine attacks. She was still a hard-working woman, a devoted mother and a wife. She had been with Pitaji through thick and thin. Her foresightedness and saving habits had given her immense wealth to lead a good life. She was still a simple housewife, who gladly helped her needy friends and relatives. Life was full of contentment and bliss but for one thing...

Amma had developed a clot in the brain, which was though not much dangerous, but yet was very vulnerable...Doctor had clearly warned Pitaji that she must not fall down backwards at any cost or it may prove fatal.

Pitaji was convinced that nothing would happen to Amma who was still mentally strong despite her failing health. She refused to take rest and convinced him that it was ok for her to do household chores. She could not find anybody doing the chores as deftly as she was doing. She cooked, washed and cleaned with her hands .Those hands worked still faster than many young ladies, who were half her age. The one thing which continuously pestered her was–cleaning... she was a perfectionist .When it came to cleaning of everything as common as a refrigerator, she cleaned the refrigerator with utmost care as if it was some rare piece of art.

...nobody had imagined that her cleanliness drive would lead her to her death bed...

Death warns us beforehand through nightmares, illusions and even omens, but we ignore all these signs as mere anxious thoughts for our loved ones.

Sometimes these death signs appear in the lives of the loved ones of the person who is about to die...may be as a warning or a direct indication.

I had always been a close aide of Amma. We were more like friends, rather than the mother-daughter duo. Like Amma, I too was a firm believer of omens.

It was late afternoon. I was fasting. It was *"karva chauth"*; The most pious fast for a married Hindu woman. I had not eaten anything since the morning except *"sargi"*, a customary early breakfast of sweets, fruits and *sewayaa*. which had to be taken before sunrise. To mark the beginning of fast, women had to give up water and food for the entire day and end their fast after seeing the moon in the sky.

I felt some pain in my head. Another attack of migraine... I thought. I dreaded it. I knew migraine attack could mean another four-five days of continuous pain. It won't subside even if I took one pain killer after another.

Migraines always remind me of my mother. 'Amma' as everybody fondly called her. Amma was known in the family for her box, full of painkillers. She took one painkiller after another. Sometimes even two together to curb her pain. While everybody was rather amused or even felt bad for her condition, it was only me who understood her pain.

Now I too was repeating the same.. I thought of Amma again. Amma had never kept the 'Karva Chauth' fast. I thought of calling her on the landline but something stopped me. I glanced at my wrist watch...it had stopped. I looked at the wall clock... it wasn't moving either. It was a bad omen for me.

'I hope Amma is all right.'

'I would call her after evening Pooja.' I thought but changed my mind the very next moment. I picked up the receiver to call but no luck... the phone was dead too.

First the wrist watch, then the wall clock and now this phone...

I felt a biting pain in my forehead as if someone had pierced a needle through my head. I sat down on the sofa holding my head with both hands.

I heard a knock on the door. It was ajar. Before I could get up, I saw my neighbor's son rushing in. He was gasping for breath as he had been running to give me an important message.

"What is the matter Arun? Is your mother ready for Pooja so early?" I asked him. As we had been doing *Karva chauth* Pooja together for many years.

"No Aunty, your brother called up to say that your mother is not well and they are taking her to the hospital", He said still panting for breath.

I knew my mother was already dead.

* * *

Omens were indeed present and shouting out loudly for Meera as well. She knew that her days were numbered. One evening she suddenly felt dizzy and became unconscious. She had felt as if she was in a dream. She was surrounded by her mother, father and her elder brother.

Meera was especially fond of her mother and her eldest brother. In her dream, she saw that they had recovered from their illness. Mother from her jaundice, Father from his psoriasis and Bhaiji from his heart stroke. Her mother then took Meera's hand and mounted her on a horseback.

Together they rode away to a beautiful grassland ahead. Meera was feeling happy in her heart to meet her parents and her elder brother after so many years. Suddenly she felt a numb pain in her head. She felt she was waking up from her dream. She could feel her pacemaker working, she could even hear heart beats…somebody was pulling her back from the horse and shaking up her shoulders. She could hear herself being called…"Amma, amma. Amma…" it was Sarjan's wife Mala who was weeping, shouting and shaking Meera's body.

"I am alright…" Meera could manage to say after opening her eyes.

Chapter 5

PREETO

I am Preeto, the second daughter of Sukhdev and Meera. "Amma" as my mother was fondly called by everyone in the family had a near death experience. It was sheer luck that Mala Aunty was nearby. She shook Amma's body with great force. It was due to this shaking that Amma was brought back to life.

For the next three months, Amma started making arrangements for her final departure from this world—the final journey, the journey of heaven. She had quickly completed her knitting work, which she had been holding up for a long time. These sweaters of all shapes and sizes were meant for her daughters and her son's children. She knew that when a person dies, his/her body is kept on a bed sheet, and not directly on the ground. She didn't trust her children to be wise and believed that they would put the newest bed sheet under her body; but such a wastage wasn't approved by her. So, she carefully pulled out an old bed sheet from her bed-box for her last ritual. Next day, she called me up. I was married in the same city, so she often called me to visit her.

"Now I am about to die soon; so don't be a fool and pull out the new bed sheet for my body, instead use this one", she said putting the old bed sheet in my hands.

I threw away the bed sheet.

"You have gone mad, Amma", I said.

* * *

I was married to Amma's closest friend Lila's son Raj. We were a happy family. I was now a mother of two sons. In spite of this, I always felt the pain of separating from my girl child whom I had named- Ritu.

Death is always painful, but it is cruelest for the family members who are left suffering after losing their loved one. It was diagnosed that I could face complications in my first pregnancy as I was underweight. Yet, I went forward with the pregnancy, gave birth to a beautiful daughter. I felt on the top of the world on the day my daughter was born…her little nose, beautiful eyes, tiny little hands; everything was like a dream come true .The joy of bringing a new life on earth can only be understood by a mother.

I never understood why my mother was so emotional. Amma had cried her heart out when I was getting married. But I was too excited to get married. New clothes and jewelry fascinated me. Amma was inconsolable and had succumbed to fits after Veera's marriage. I felt relieved to know that I was getting married to someone already known to her. That meant I could visit Amma as many times as I wanted because Lila -my mother-in-law, understood her friend's mental condition.

However, things had changed after Ritu was born. The family was expecting a boy. But I and my husband cared for no one. We were too happy with our bundle of joy. Ultimately, my family too embraced our daughter.

When Ritu turned six month old, she developed a rather poor digestion. She would vomit frequently. We consulted every doctor, but Ritu's condition deteriorated with time. One day she succumbed to her illness.

I was still holding little Ritu in my arms, vigorously rubbing her feet and hands, which felt cold as ice. Doctor checked her pulse, she was no more. We were dumbfounded. How could God be so cruel? Why was our daughter snatched away by destiny?

Why? Why?

I won't let go of the dead body of Ritu. I was still holding her tightly to my bosom. So, I had to be sedated while Raj carried away the tiny body to perform the last rites.

When finally I woke up, I found myself in the lap of Amma. I knew my life would never be the same without my daughter Ritu.

"Amma, Ritu has gone", I said wiping my tears. "Promise me that you will never leave me alone...", I said hiding myself in Amma's arms.

Since that incident, I visited my mother every alternate day to check that she was ok. Though I had been blessed with two sons after Ritu's death, I understood that the bond which a mother shares with her daughter, cannot be compared to any other relationship in the world.

Now when Amma had suddenly started talking about her death, the fear of losing her after losing my daughter shuddered my soul.

Chapter 6

MEERA'S DEATH

It was rather a cold and cloudy morning of early November. The winter season had just tip-toed. It was still not powerful enough to induce people to wear any warm clothing. The grey clouds look sad though it was a day of festival; especially for all the married ladies, it was the 'karva chauth' festival. On this very festival, every married woman of India keeps a fast for the entire day, without even drinking a drop of water till she sees the moon and prays to God to give a long and a healthy life to her husband.

Though Meera had never observed a fast as it was not prevalent in Pakistan but she had never stopped her daughter–in–law Priya from embracing new customs and traditions of 'Hindustani culture'. With great enthusiasm she had called a 'choori walah' at her home so that her daughter-in-law could choose colorful bangles to wear with her sari on this occasion. He had bangles of all colours and sizes... some were of metal, some of glass and some made from plastic. Priya selected glass bangles of pink and blue colour.

The 'choori walah' was eager to sell more bangles so he insisted that Meera should also purchase some bangles for herself...but she politely refused ;instead she bought four more pairs from him. These were for her daughters who were expected to visit soon during the upcoming winter vacations.

It was the middle of the afternoon and the sun was still playing hide and seek with the clouds. Everyone in the house was feeling a bit lazy after lunch and the children were watching TV lying on the sofa. Priya and Gyan went to their room upstairs to take some rest. Sukhdev took up morning paper and decided to re-read it ... in case he had missed something...

Meera was not feeling lazy at all and decided to clean the refrigerator instead of taking a short nap. As she was squatting down on the floor, she lost her balance and fell backwards with her head banging the floor...she was still conscious as she remembered what the doctor had warned about the clot in her head...she must never fall down...she was losing breath..., maybe either the pacemaker had stopped working... or she had a nervous breakdown...the pictures blurred as she heard shrieking voices of her grandchildren... one of them had rushed to call her son...she was lying in her son's arms... but slowly everything faded away...

Meera was rushed to hospital but there was no sign of life on her face which had grown pale. Everyone in the house was dumbfounded about the incident. It was like a big blow on their face. Suddenly the support system of the house was pulled away, and that too abruptly... No time was given to Sukhdev by the evil fate to think what had happened. He returned back home with the dead body. She was laid on the floor on a new bed sheet which she had been insisting not to put beneath her when she might die...!

Sukhdev did not know how to react...he was still not believing that his dear wife had suddenly left him without even talking to him in the final moments. He saw his black diary lying on the *table....it was a new journal which he had been gifted last month by a client so that he could record some important events in it. He was just getting used to the habit of journaling...his mind being the only journal for the past so many years.*

He quietly turned to the page which mentioned the date: 4th November, 2000. He wrote one line with shaking hands: Meera Devi died from nerve clot and cardiac arrest.

Chapter 7

VIRAAJ—THE SECOND GENERATION

Amidst a large office, sits Sukhdev with his back facing a mosaic of brown tiles, which are carved out delicately. Towards his left is another cabin used for conferences. The right-side and front walls are partly covered with wooden shelves which store an infinite number of books, papers and files. He is discussing something avidly with a client who is seated on a leather sofa in front of him. Though Sukhdev has grown quite old by his looks, yet no one could still compete with him when it came to remembering rules, regulations, amendments, new tax laws and benefits, etc.

The client seems to be in awe of him as he deftly explains another regulation quoting from a newly opened book. His staff has yet not gone through it, but Sukhdev has already memorized the latest changes made by the excise department. The client nods, he appears satisfied and in safe hands. With such an experienced man, trust comes automatically and when someone trusts you...business is a matter too obvious.

As the clock struck four, the client decided to leave as he had to travel a long distance back to his home. He then took leave from Sukhdev again reconfirming his faith and with extreme gratitude in his eyes. The office clerk came in with a file and a bunch of papers, which he had been working upon. These were the important documents on which he needed to discuss with Sukhdev.

Not a moment of respite for an old man like him...the clerk thought as he took pity on his own hectic schedule. Of course he was not a workaholic like his boss, and surely would prefer a quite retired life watching TV and doing yoga if he could help it.

But Sukhdev had exactly different thinking patterns. He was for sure a workaholic but not by choice. Life had been too hard on him but he had never bowed down to its atrocities, and by his sheer hard work, had not only sustained but created a passion for life and work. He had never shared his feelings with anyone before. It was only his wife Meera, who could understand him without uttering any word. Now that she was no longer his companion his work had turned out to be his soulmate, which wrapped up most of his time so that he had nothing else left in his mind to think about.

The clerk left, placing the files on the table. Once again Sukhdev got busy in studying them. He is so focused on his work that he does not hear the knock on his door or is it his age, which is playing games with his body... but age has yet not deterred his will power which is as strong as it was during the partition.

It is his grandson Viraaj who enters the office. He knows his grandfather is too busy to look up.

"Pitaji"

These words were enough to bring him back to life from the world of infinite lines and pages. He looked up; he knew everyone fondly addressed him by this name only. Though it stands for 'father' but he has been a fatherly figure to me his grandson and almost all the relatives address him as "Pitaji".

Seeing me in front of him always filled him with happiness and fear simultaneously. He believed that his grandchildren had lost their mother at this stage of life, when they were ready to open their wings and explore the world. Though she fought bravely with her Cancer, but gave up when it struck her body again and again spreading its claws to all the vital organs of her body. For almost fifteen years, my sister and I had witnessed our mother battling against it, but there comes a time when almost everyone is prepared for the inevitable...

I had inherited the height and eyes of my mother, like her I had big black eyes with a towering height of over six feet. I was a chubby kid once but now it appeared that every part of flesh had vanished from my body, leaving behind a well-toned body which gave me a muscular look. I had become more serious towards life after losing both my mother and my grandmother. I was full of enthusiasm for my work.

"Have you taken your lunch Pitaji?", I asked.

No, but never mind we will skip lunch today as I had a lot of tea since morning, and I am not feeling hungry anymore."

"But you must eat something before we go out to meet the client; it is almost two-hour journey"

"Don't worry, I will be ok. You just go downstairs and wait for me in the car, I will be there in five minutes", Pitaji replied hastily looking at the papers.

I was quite concerned about my grandfather who was a workaholic. His age demanded him to take adequate rest, sleep and food at proper times. But with no woman in the house to nag him for his food, he had grown quite weak. He had pain while walking and sometimes his left foot went numb, so he had to forcibly put it down on the ground for taking the next step.

I knew about this, so I proposed to stay with him till he completed his work. It took another fifteen minutes for Pitaji to complete his work. Now, we were ready to leave... on an empty stomach.

After a long and a bumpy journey which was marked by constant traffic jams and erratic weather, we finally reached our destination. It was raining cats and dogs and we could not escape getting wet within seconds of leaving our car. Pitaji felt awfully perspired and hot though he could not understand whether it was the rain or his own sweat in which he was drenched.

"Are you ok Pitaji?" I looked at my grandfather who was struggling with stairs at the entrance.

Pitaji was able to nod only...he found his strength leaving him. A sudden pang of pain attacked his left arm and chest.

However, he felt better once we were inside the air conditioned office of the new client.

"Are you ok sir?" asked Mr. Bakshi, the new client.

"He looks pale and needs some rest", I urged.

"No, no it's ok" Pitaji pleaded as he did not want to waste all the time we had taken to reach here and after all Mr. Bakshi was a very busy man. He had been a friend of Pitaji's senior in the department and it was through reference that we were able to fix a meeting with him today.

"Please have some water..." Mr. Bakshi was just handing over the glass to Pitaji, when he collapsed on the chair.

Years of toil and hard work had slowly been taxing his body. The body was in dire need of rest due to old age, but it was surprisingly stout... it needed a little nourishment only proper meals at the proper time and medicines, to support the whole system.

Doctors diagnosed it as a minor heart attack, but warned him against stressing too much and going back to work was strictly prohibited. He needed complete rest with a proper diet schedule.

After getting discharged from the hospital after one week, Pitaji was rather nervous about going back to home.

How would he cope up?

He had many tasks still left in his schedule...he could not think of taking rest now, when it was time to support me: his grandson in my business, but his health and weakness were still bothering him.

* * *

The extended family came once again to our rescue. I was absolutely gratified by the caring and concern shown by my aunts and uncles, who took upon the task to look after Pitaji's food and other necessities. My fatherGyan had to keep his job and he was not in a position to take leave from his office, though he wanted to look after his ailing father.

My father had lost his mother and his wife in a short span of ten years, since then the burden of running the house and raising up kids had fallen on his shoulders.

* * *

The forced rest period was working nicely on my grandfather's body, which was not habitual to such a practice but nevertheless he was recovering quickly in spite of his age.

The doctors said it was his will power which was giving him strength against all odds. At the time when people of his age had long retired, rather forgotten that they had ever worked in their life, he was ready to start afresh.

Chapter 8

SUKHDEV

It was a cold winter day with rain lashing around the trees and wind making a rumbling noise. I was being examined by my friend cum Doctor- Dr. Vishnu. We were almost of the same age. The doctor too had lost his wife... though more violently in a car accident. His duty as a doctor was the only thing which had saved him from succumbing to heart disease or any other ailment, which was so obvious at this age.

"It will be getting colder..." I said looking out of the window. The clouds had turned sinister, blocking away any form of sunlight.

"Yes, you are right my friend", replied Dr. Vishnu

"Dr. Saab, what should I do now to keep myself busy? The thought of retiring has never occurred to me. I have always believed in living an active life."

"Yes, that is the first thing which should be very important for you. I will not encourage you to leave your active life, but switch to something, which gives satisfaction to your heart...

Something that you can relate to...something which has been long pending in your mind, but you never had the time or resources to do so".

"Tell me" he said bending over the X-ray report he was reading, "When you were running away from Pakistan what were your thoughts? What did you pray for ?"

"I never cared about myself, it was the wellbeing of my family which bothered me a lot", I replied with my eyes fixed on a distant cloud as if it was a witness to my hard days.

"All I thought about was finding a shelter for my mother, we were tired of travelling and sleeping in refugee camps. I wanted to continue my education because I loved to study, but I had nobody to help me. If Baba would not have been there, I could have never made it through my school and college. Today, I would have been an uneducated, unskilled labour who has to fight for his daily wages and two square meals", I said, closing my eyes.

"...What will give me satisfaction, ok let me think about it. Now that you have mentioned ...I will think over your suggestion", I said coming back to my senses.

It was already dark and cold, when I came out of the hospital. I made myself comfortable, nodded the driver to move the vehicle. We were now on the main road, I could see homeless people spreading out their tattered blankets to get ready for sleep under the flyover. I suddenly thought of Ram Singh–a daily wager whom I had once met in Delhi.

I was in the habit of walking during my lunch break. Once construction work was going on in the outer premises of the airport terminal, so I decided to walk over to that area; it was here that I first met Ram Singh. Once Ram Singh had protected me from a falling beam, since then we had become good friends.

I was moved by the harsh life which Ram Singh was living. He was homeless and it was like a third degree torture to survive during the cold winter months. He had narrated how he slept under the bridge during night with a tattered blanket and some fire, which he made by burning scrap lying around the road. In the middle of the night, they were poked mercilessly by the patrolling policemen. If any theft occurred in that area, they were the first ones to be picked up by the police. They were tortured, beaten up and paraded before the complainant. Some of them served as drivers, cleaners, maids to the nearby houses, yet their employers never cared to protect them if they were held by police. Though the government had created night shelters, but they didn't want to sleep there. Such places were full of foul smells of liquor, vomit and urine. Women too were vulnerable to rape and abduction. Due to this reason Ram Singh had kept his family safe at his native village, which he visited once in three years.

I had tried to help him but one day the construction work was handed over to the new contractor, since then Ram Singh never returned to work. I felt like I had lost a friend who was in need of help...

* * *

I was in the hospital for almost one week. Now that I was back to my home, something else bothered me. During my stay at the hospital a mishap had occurred. Several school children had been admitted to the school after eating their mid-day meals. These were poor children belonging to the slum areas. Their parents could not afford to feed them twice a day; so the government had decided to provide them with an afternoon meal. In another incident, the water provided to the residents of a colony was so bad that many people suffered from diarrhea, jaundice and few of them died as they could not afford to drink clean water. This reminded me of the refugee camps during partition. I had seen many people die due to contaminated water. Then, I was a helpless lad who believed that he had just lost his father. Though, today I had actually lost my father, but I was not helpless.

I had once been a part of the system. I understood fully that red tapism and age-old laws were shielding the guilty; while the Government posed itself as helpless. As I lay on my bed watching TV; I was impressed by a veteran Gandhian who declared indefinite fast to enforce a new regulation. People were on the streets shouting against the Government, hunger strikes, and candle marches were going on while he was on his 'forced' bed rest. How eagerly I wanted to join them!!

Something inside me was boiling. I also wanted to be a part of this. I wanted to feel the energy of the masses when they were out facing water cannons, police beating them with lathis. The thought of my days in Pakistan, and the bloody partition crossed my minds and started haunting me. I could not do anything then, because I was a kid. I could not stand against the so-called politicians when the partition was announced. I could not ask them who was to take responsibility for thousands of people who lost their homes, their families while a Britisher decided to tear off a part of one land from another, casually, moving his blue pencil over a lifeless map. But now, I was a bonafide citizen of this country. I had the right and might to stand against the wrong-doers.

After two months of complete rest, I had already made up my mind to work for the society. I disclosed my intention of contesting the local elections to my children. Nobody liked the idea, not because they feared that I would fail, but they feared for my health. While my grandson wanted me to help him in his business, my daughters wanted me to take rest and not divulge in 'bloody politics', which was too time consuming and could prove costly to my health. But, I had made up my mind. Now for the first time in my life, I had thought about myself. It had always been family first, but now when I no longer had the burden to look after my parents, sisters, daughters, wife and grandchildren—all were busy in their own lives; now was the time to turn a new leaf from the chapter of life.

"I am still not over, now is the time to give back to society", I told them.

* * *

The evening had just begun to set in the orange sky. It was getting cold once again, and I had called up everybody in the house to sit with me in the living room. I had been pondering on his decision for quite some time now. It was time to seek advice from my family members too.

"What is it? "What are you thinking so seriously?", Viraaj was first to ask.

"I am thinking of doing something to help homeless people in our neighborhood ..."

"You have not even fully recovered from your illness and you want to go for social service?", Veera expressed her apprehension.

"Yes, Pitaji, I agree with *didi*", Gyan said

"No, no let me complete first…it has been my desire to do something for my society and for our country", I pleaded.

"When I worked as a Government servant all my life, I tried to be as honest as possible to serve this country, which has not given me birth but it is my motherland, and I owe my life to it."

"It has been a very long time since I left Pakistan...but those images of massacre still eclipse my mind. Even though I am thankful to God for everything which He has given me, yet I feel incomplete. Our scriptures and holy books have always taught us that true happiness lies in serving the people selflessly, and that is exactly what my heart desires now."

I narrated to them my near death experience, when I was on the operation table. For a moment I felt so light, just like a leaf floating ...I had no body and yet I had my memories. The story of my entire life appeared to me in flashes...then I was blinded by a white light, it was very soothing and cool. Just like the river flowing down the mountains.

Then I heard a question: "did you live well?"

I realized that my entire life had been full of acts which I did for my family, my friends and my loved ones. Never in my life I had shown kindness to any stranger or the beggar or the crippled man whom I had seen many times. I had always believed them to be crooks looking for sympathy and money of foolish people. Those who dropped a coin or two into their dirty hands were considered emotional fools by me.

I had never been an optimist, rather I was well known for my skepticism. I had seen so much in life that I had turned critical over everything and even on trivial matters, my opinion was that—everything and everyone was 'hopeless'. I was a pessimist but I was never violent or dominating. I expressed my opinion and then moved out of the scene. I was the head of the family but it was Meera, who actually ran the house with her commanding nature and stern voice. Despite all these feelings, I was full of compassion for my grandchildren.

I finally decided to build a night shelter for the homeless children and elderly. It was just the onset of winters, and I had seen several street children sleeping at the open spaces below the flyovers. I had also seen people distributing woolen blankets to them, but it was impossible to sleep properly in that extreme cold weather. I had a childhood friend who was now a wealthy jeweler-Lala Deen Dayal. Lalaji as he was fondly called by his children, was now retired from his active business life, so he was the perfect partner and investor for my ideas...

Chapter 9

LALA JI

I have been a good friend of Sukhdev for thirty years. We met when my family was shifting to Haryana from a small village in Punjab. We had been extremely lucky and that's why we survived the massacre of partition.

It so happened that we had a flourishing gold business in Lahore. My father's business partners were settled in Punjab and Delhi. I was very young at the time of partition, almost of Sukhdev's age. My uncle would come frequently to Delhi from Lahore. He would then visit his extended family in Punjab.

Being a regular in the political circles of Delhi, one of the goldsmiths warned him of the consequences of Independence. He also informed us about the partition. Of course, we treated this news as fake. But he insisted that we should at least move the women folk out of Lahore timely.

My father was a very cautious man. There was an upcoming

marriage function in Delhi; he asked that all women should be taken to Delhi without any delay. As it was a grand marriage, so he asked the ladies to carry their jewelry along with lots of clothes, cash and other valuables with them. Little children too accompanied their mothers. Women were not told about the partition.

Only my uncles and father stayed back in Lahore. I had accompanied women folk to look after their needs in Delhi. After the marriage was over, we moved to our extended family in Punjab. By then, the massacre had started. Soon my uncles and my father joined us in Punjab. In this way, we were able to save our families and our precious gold.

I set up a jewelry shop along with my father in Delhi. The competition was stiff. Delhi was flooded with refugees. We too had to move out of Delhi. Finally, we relocated to Gurgaon and set up our shops. Gradually, our family too shifted from Punjab to Gurgaon. Since then, it had maintained a high reputation, and we became wealthiest amongst the refugee community.

When I met Sukhdev, I found that we had nothing in common. He was educated, a highly placed Government officer; I was an uneducated jeweler. He wore shirt- pants, while I stuck to my white dhoti-kurta with a matching white turban. Even our body complexions were opposite. Sukhdev was surprisingly light skinned while I was dusky. As we say, opposites attract each other, maybe this was the reason that we grew fond of each other in no time.

Sukhdev was an honest man. When he was getting his eldest daughter married, he had not much savings left to give her gold. But still he chose the very best jewelry for her. I assured him that he could buy anything from my shop. I trusted him blindly. Such was our friendship.

As time passed on, we both got busy in bringing up our children, then our grandchildren. We lost touch with each other.

Now, after so many years Sukhdev has reconnected with me. He has an interesting project for society. The energy and enthusiasm which I had witnessed in him thirty years ago, has sparkled up again. The light is shining in those eyes again. Whatever be the project... I just want to feel that camaraderie again.

* * *

Sukhdev had never realized that he could be so energetic at this stage of life. Soon the project of night shelter took off. He was now even busier than ever. Every morning I would reach at his doorstep and after sipping a cup of tea, we geared up for collecting donations. We were in our early 70s but we looked like a pair of enthusiastic school kids on a mission. The smile and the shine on our faces was enough to tell that we were thoroughly enjoying this 'responsibility.'

Sukhdev was amazed how nicely people treated him. He never knew that he was so popular among the people of his community. He realized that people respected him a lot. He also felt ashamed of himself as he had turned off many such visitors who asked for donations from him. It pained him to recollect how he had been sarcastic towards a few of them...

It took us six months and hundreds of odd hours to finally collect the required amount for the construction of the night shelter; the remaining amount was to be jointly contributed by Sukhdev and me. Few small rooms were created, which served as classes for teaching the street children. People were happy that some useful work was going on in their neighborhood, and many people came forward to teach these distressed children. The night shelter was also successful.

Above all, Sukhdev felt an immense calm and happiness to see his dream fulfilled. Now that he had completed it, it gave him confidence that his life could be useful to the society. He had always been a hard-working man. He never shied away from his responsibilities. But toiling day and night for the well-being of his family was something of a responsibility, which never gave him inner satisfaction. However, now the feeling was totally different...this bliss was something which he had never experienced before.

Unknowingly, this project had made him immensely popular among the people of this area. They had started considering him as a father figure and a potential leader in making. The assembly elections were close and people urged him to contest elections as an independent candidate. Sukhdev had been a Government official for years, and he was well versed with the red tapism of offices and the Government.

He thought that it could be a good way to help people. On second thoughts...he knew politics was a dirty game. He will be facing a lot of criticism from some groups, they may also call him an opportunist and even his family could be at risk. All these thoughts were disturbing him day and night.

He was in a dilemma.

Meanwhile, he received news about the illness of his mother. She was growing old with her advanced age, but still had hope in her eyes. She had always wished to bring back the lost fame and the family name in this country-Hindustan, which was now her home.

Chapter 10

BHAGONWALI

Sukhdev had to leave his election campaign midway to visit me. I didn't want to disturb him. Now, he had a bigger responsibility. That was to serve as a citizen of this motherland-Hindustan, The land which was now ours. It had given us food, shelter, and a name, protected our lives.

He could not stay with me for long, as it was the last day of campaign. His responsibilities as a dutiful son were now at stake. He knew I would understand him. Of course, I had never been a nagging or bothersome mother, but now I was really old. This had caused me to forget about things and people. In Spite of all this, I talked about Sukhdev almost every day to whoever would care to listen. I loved him a lot.

It was on the day when the election result was to be declared.

Sukhdev decided he would bring me back to his home.

"Bibi, do you recognize me ?", Sukhdev asked me, holding my trembling fingers.

"Sukhdev, my son...you have come, finally you have come", I said giving a toothless smile. In spite of all efforts of Sukhdev, I had refused to stay with him. I believed that my younger son was immature and needed me more. After Meera was gone, I had nobody in Sukhdev's house who could be my companion. His daughter-in-law was already suffering from cancer. How could I be a burden on her?

Things were different now.

I realized that I was useless for anybody. I had lost my husband and now it was my turn to join him. I had a diminished memory. I had sudden episodes of partition in front of my eyes that would make me go into panic attacks and cry for help. I developed insomnia and depression. Sometimes I kept on repeating the same words. It was really pathetic.

"Now I want to take Bibi with me, and you will not try to stop her with any of your tantrums," Sukhdev said in a stern voice to his brother.

"Take her. I will not say a word" was the cold remark that he received from his brother.

Without wasting another moment he picked up all my medicines and doctor's prescriptions and carried my withered frame into his car.

Sukhdev was already feeling a sense of achievement when he was taking me home. He was happy that now he could spend some time with me. The campaign work was completed, so only the result was awaited.

"Sukkhi..."

"Yes, Bibi do you want anything?"

"You have been a dutiful son, husband and a father...you are just like your Baba", I said motioning him to sit beside me.

"Why do you talk like this? I am not a good son or else I would have never let you stay with Rajje..." Sukhdev was feeling angry at himself.

"He is just a stupid little boy, he cannot even wipe his nose...see that is why Baba wants me to stay with him..." I was lost in time again.

"Now I don't have much time left, I am happy that I will be dying in your lap. Perhaps that was the reason I had been holding on till this long or else your Baba comes to me every day...you know what he says..."

Tears rolled out from Sukhdev's eyes but I was lost in thoughts.

The driver set his foot on the brake and with a creaking sound the car came to a halt. Sukhdev carried me in his arms out of the car in spite of the immense pain in his legs. He placed my body on the bed with utmost care.

He ordered the servants to call the doctor.

"Bibi, will you eat something ?"

"Give me a few drops of Gangajal... I motioned the servant. Sukhdev gave him a nod.

"Here, take it..." Sukhdev raised my head with his arm and placed the spoon on my wrinkled lips.

My eyes were full of gratitude. I smiled at him.

"Don't cry, don't worry about me... see who has come..." I pointed towards the door.

Sukhdev was bewildered as he could not see anyone. But I could see my husband standing in the doorway, ready to take me along with him.

Sukhdev realized that his mother was now ready to die. I was smiling and talking in soft whispers to his Baba who was now standing at my bedside. But he was totally invisible to Sukhdev.

"Sukkhi...now I must leave, I promised your Baba that I will die in your lap. You have been a very dutiful son. I pray to God that he showers his blessings on you."

For the last time I ran my old fingers on his forehead and his head as if blessing him finally and then I closed my eyes forever.

As my soul departed from my body, I could see that my son was in shock.

Sukhdev sat there holding my frame in his arms, looking at me as my body slept peacefully. There was a smile on my face and in spite of my wrinkles my body looked...beautiful. He knew his mother was dead, his tears knew that, as they now flowed non stop from his eyes, he felt like shouting at the top of his voice but he only sobbed slowly like a child who thinks that his demand will be fulfilled, if he shows his crying face to his mother. He was still hopeful that there was some life left in me.

He shook my body but it didn't quiver.

His phone bell rang continuously. The party workers had assembled outside his home with crackers and sweets. It was time to celebrate. His hard work had been fruitful.

He had won the elections by a heavy margin.

This was my last gift to my son.

May you always shine.

✦✦✦

CALL TO ACTION

After teaching my readers almost everything about Fear that is worth knowing, I want to make you all immune to this menace.

No matter, whether you have mild symptoms of getting engulfed with fear, or you are asymptomatic, you will get freedom for sure.

You can connect with me at:

📞 011-41050054

✉️ kanika@cargopeople.com

🌐 cargopeople.com

📷 k.Adlakha

🐦 @pingaksh Kanika adlakha

📘 kanika.adlakha.31

And express your urge to make appointment with me.

Writing the Book Alone on this subject was never my dream.

My dream was to make you immune to this success-obstructing, depressing, life intimidating emotion.

Come and Join me to Drive Fear out of your Mind!!

Notes:

Notes: